POCKET CHEF

Slow Cooking

igloobooks

igloobooks

Published in 2016
by Igloo Books Ltd
Cottage Farm
Sywell
NN6 0BJ
www.igloobooks.com

Food photography and recipe development:
© Stockfood, The Food Media Agency
Cover image © Stockfood, The Food Media Agency

HUN001 0216
2 4 6 8 10 9 7 5 3 1
ISBN 978-1-78557-531-0

Cover designed by Nicholas Gage
Interiors designed by Charles Wood-Penn
Edited by Caroline Icke

Printed and manufactured in China

Contents

Soups

Squash and Pine Nut Soup

SERVES 6

PREPARATION TIME **10 MINUTES**

COOKING TIME **4 HOURS**

INGREDIENTS

1 large butternut squash, peeled, deseeded and
    cut into chunks
1 onion, finely chopped
2 cloves of garlic, finely chopped
1 tsp ground cumin
1 litre / 1 pint 15 fl. oz / 4 cups vegetable stock
3 tbsp pine nuts
2 tbsp chives, chopped
salt and pepper

METHOD

1. Mix the squash with the onion, garlic and
   cumin in a slow cooker, then pour over the
   stock and season with salt and pepper.

2. Cover the slow cooker and cook on high
   for 4 hours. Use a potato masher or stick
   blender to break down the squash into
   a purée.

3. Toast the pine nuts in a dry frying pan
   for 2 minutes or until golden, stirring
   frequently.

4. Ladle the soup into warm bowls, then
   sprinkle with the pine nuts and chives.

TOP TIP
This soup is also
delicious made with
sweet potatoes.

Slow-cooked Spring Vegetable Minestrone

SERVES 4

PREPARATION TIME 5 MINUTES

COOKING TIME 1 HOUR 30 MINUTES

INGREDIENTS

1.2 litres / 2 pints / 4 ¾ cups vegetable stock

100 g / 3 ½ oz / 1 cup dried spaccatelle or similar pasta shapes

12 asparagus spears, cut into short lengths

1 courgette (zucchini), sliced

4 spring onions (scallions), chopped

2 medium tomatoes, peeled and chopped

3 tbsp pesto

50 g / ¾ oz piece of Parmesan

METHOD

1. Put the stock, pasta, asparagus and courgette in a slow cooker and cook on medium for 1 hour 30 minutes.

2. Stir in the tomatoes and pesto, then ladle into warm bowls and shave the Parmesan over the top with a vegetable peeler.

TOP TIP

Try stirring sliced smoked salmon through the soup just before serving.

Fish Soup

SERVES 4

PREPARATION TIME 15–20 MINUTES

COOKING TIME 3 HOURS 15 MINUTES

INGREDIENTS

30 ml / 1 fl. oz / 2 tbsp olive oil
2 cloves garlic, minced
2 bulbs fennel, trimmed and finely chopped
300 g / 10 ½ oz / 2 cups prawns, peeled
    and deveined
2 x 200 g / 7 oz sea bass fillets,
    pin-boned and cut into large chunks
500 ml / 18 fl. oz / 2 cups fish stock
250 ml / 9 fl. oz / 1 cup passata
55 ml / 2 fl. oz / ¼ cup Cognac
30 g / 1 oz / ¼ cup fresh breadcrumbs
2 sprigs of tarragon
1 tbsp extra-virgin olive oil
salt and pepper

METHOD

1. Heat the olive oil in a large saucepan set over a moderate heat until hot and sweat the garlic and fennel for 5-6 minutes, stirring occasionally until softened.

2. Deglaze the saucepan with the Cognac, letting it reduce by half.

3. Spoon everything from the saucepan into a slow cooker and add all the remaining ingredients apart from the extra-virgin olive oil and the breadcrumbs.

4. Cook on a low setting for 3 hours until the fish and seafood is tender and cooked; the soup should be thickened.

5. Puree using a stick blender until smooth.

6. If the soup is thin, thicken using the fresh breadcrumbs then adjust the seasoning to taste using the olive oil, salt and pepper.

7. Ladle into warm soup bowls before garnishing.

TOP TIP
Leave the soup unblended for a chunky texture and leave out the breadcrumbs.

Creamy Beetroot Soup

SERVES 4

PREPARATION TIME **15 MINUTES**

COOKING TIME **3 HOURS**

INGREDIENTS

1.2 litres / 2 pints / 4 ¾ cups vegetable stock
450 g / 1 lb / 3 cups beetroot, peeled and sliced
1 bay leaf
2 tsp cumin seeds, plus extra for sprinkling
150 ml / 5 ½ fl. oz / ⅔ cup double (heavy) cream
salt and pepper

METHOD

1. Put the stock, beetroot, bay leaf and cumin seeds in a slow cooker. Cover and cook on high for 3 hours.

2. Discard the bay leaf and reserve a few slices of beetroot to garnish, then ladle the rest into a liquidizer and blend until smooth.

3. Stir in two thirds of the cream and season to taste with salt and pepper.

4. Pour the soup into four warm bowls, then scatter over the reserved beetroot, drizzle with the rest of the cream and sprinkle with cumin seeds.

TOP TIP

Try garnishing the soup with crumbled feta for a tangy finish.

Haricot and Coriander Soup

SERVES 4

PREPARATION TIME 25 MINUTES

COOKING TIME 8 HOURS

INGREDIENTS

400 g / 14 oz / 2 ⅔ cups dried haricot beans,
   soaked overnight
1 onion, chopped
1 celery stick, chopped
2 tsp coriander (cilantro) seeds, crushed,
   plus extra for sprinkling
4 cloves of garlic, sliced
2 tbsp coriander (cilantro) leaves, chopped

METHOD

1. Drain the beans from their soaking water
   and put them in a large saucepan of cold
   water. Bring to the boil and cook for
   10 minutes, then drain well.

2. Mix the beans with the onion, celery,
   coriander seeds and garlic in a slow
   cooker. Pour over enough boiling water
   to cover everything by 5 cm (2 in), then
   cook on low for 8 hours.

3. Season to taste with salt and pepper,
   then blend until smooth in a liquidizer.

4. Ladle into warm bowls and garnish with
   coriander leaves and crushed coriander
   seeds before serving.

TOP TIP

This soup is also delicious garnished with pieces of crispy bacon.

Bollywood Soup

SERVES 4

PREPARATION TIME **15 MINUTES**

COOKING TIME **40 MINUTES**

INGREDIENTS

3 tbsp vegetable oil
1 onion, peeled and finely sliced
2 cloves of garlic, chopped
1 red chilli (chili), deseeded and finely chopped
1 tsp fresh ginger, grated
1 tsp ground coriander
pinch turmeric
½ tsp ground cumin
½ tsp garam masala
1 tsp paprika
1 tsp mustard seeds
2 sweet potatoes, peeled and chopped
450 g / 1 lb / 2 cups chicken thigh meat,
    skinned and diced
400 ml / 14 fl. oz / 1 ½ cups canned coconut milk
300 ml / 10 fl. oz / 1 ¼ cups chicken stock
coriander leaves, to garnish

METHOD

1. Heat the oil in a pan and sauté the onion for about 10 minutes or until golden-brown. Add the garlic, chilli and ginger and fry for another minute.

2. Add the spices and stir well, then add the chicken and sweet potatoes to the sauce and pour in the coconut milk and stock. Cook at a simmer for around 20 minutes until the chicken and sweet potatoes are tender.

3. Adjust the seasoning and sprinkle with coriander leaves before serving.

TOP TIP
For extra bling add diced vari-coloured peppers.

Minestrone with Turkey

METHOD

1. Put the stock, pasta, beans and peas in a slow cooker and cook on medium for 1 hour 30 minutes.

2. Add salt and pepper to taste, then ladle into warm bowls. Add ½ tbsp of pesto to each bowl, then use a vegetable peeler to shave over the pecorino. Garnish with turkey ham and serve immediately.

SERVES 4

PREPARATION TIME 10 MINUTES

COOKING TIME 1 HOUR 30 MINUTES

INGREDIENTS

1.2 litres / 2 pints / 4 ¾ cups turkey stock
100 g / 3 ½ oz / 1 cup dried gomiti or similar pasta shapes
4 runner beans, chopped
200 g / 7 oz / 1 ⅓ cups broad beans
100 g / 3 ½ oz / ⅔ cup peas
2 tbsp pesto
25 g / 1 oz / ¼ cup piece of pecorino
4 slices turkey ham, torn into pieces
salt and pepper

TOP TIP
Try using small strips of prosciutto instead of the turkey ham.

Wonton Soup

SERVES 6

PREPARATION TIME 45 MINUTES

COOKING TIME 6 HOURS 30 MINUTES

INGREDIENTS

1 chicken carcass
8 spring onions (scallions), roughly chopped
5 cm (2 in) piece fresh root ginger, sliced
1 lemon grass stem, roughly chopped
dark soy sauce to taste
3 heads pak choi, quartered
coriander (cilantro) leaves to garnish

For the wontons
150 g / 5 ½ oz / 1 cup minced chicken
75 g / 2 ½ oz / ½ cup raw prawns, finely chopped
2 cloves of garlic, crushed
1 tsp fresh root ginger, finely grated
2 spring onions (scallions), finely chopped
1 red chilli (chili), finely chopped
2 tbsp coriander (cilantro), finely chopped
1 tbsp light soy sauce
24 wonton wrappers

METHOD

1. Put the chicken carcass, spring onions, ginger and lemon grass in a slow cooker and add enough cold water to cover.

2. Cover and cook on low for 6 hours, then pass the broth through a coffee filter lined sieve to clarify. Season to taste with dark soy sauce.

3. While the broth is cooking, mix the minced chicken with the prawns, garlic, ginger, spring onion, chilli and coriander. Stir in the soy sauce. Divide the filling between the wonton wrappers, then fold them in half and press firmly to seal. Fold the edges round and crimp together.

4. Wash and dry the slow cooker and pour in the broth. Cook on high until it starts to simmer, then add the wontons and pak choi. Cover and cook for 15 minutes or until the wontons have all started to float and the pak choi stalks are just tender.

5. Ladle into warm bowls and garnish with coriander leaves.

TOP TIP
You can also use fresh scallops in place of the prawns.

SOUPS

Mussel Chowder

SERVES 4

PREPARATION TIME 15 MINUTES

COOKING TIME 1 HOUR

INGREDIENTS

2 shallots, finely chopped
2 cloves of garlic, crushed
175 ml / 6 fl. oz / ⅔ cup dry white wine
1.2 litres / 2 pints / 4 ¾ cups live mussels,
    scrubbed
500 ml / 17 ½ fl. oz / 2 cups fish stock
250 ml / 9 fl. oz / 1 cup double (heavy) cream
1 tbsp flat leaf parsley, chopped
salt and pepper

METHOD

1. Put all of the ingredients except for the cream and parsley in a slow cooker and cook on medium for 1 hour.

2. Scoop out the mussels with a slotted spoon and place in a bowl. Stir the cream into the slow cooker, cover and continue to cook. Meanwhile, pick the mussel meat from the shells, leaving a few whole for a garnish.

3. Stir the mussel meat into the soup and season to taste with salt and pepper.

4. Ladle into warm bowls and garnish with the parsley and reserved mussels in their shells.

TOP TIP
Try using a mixture of clams and mussels.

Lettuce Soup

METHOD

1. Stir everything together in a slow cooker, then cook on low for 1 hour.

2. Taste the soup for seasoning and adjust with salt and pepper, then ladle into bowls and serve.

SERVES 6

PREPARATION TIME 5 MINUTES

COOKING TIME 1 HOUR

INGREDIENTS

1.2 litres / 2 pints / 5 cups vegetable stock
1 iceberg lettuce, chopped
1 carrot, coarsely grated
100 g / 3 ½ oz / 1 ⅓ cups button mushrooms, sliced
a small bunch of chives, cut into short lengths
salt and pepper

TOP TIP
This soup also tastes great served chilled in the summer.

French Onion Soup

SERVES 4

PREPARATION TIME **10 MINUTES**

COOKING TIME **7 HOURS**

INGREDIENTS

2 tbsp butter
3 onions, quartered and sliced
2 cloves of garlic, sliced
1 tbsp balsamic vinegar
1 tbsp runny honey
1 tbsp plain (all-purpose) flour
125 ml / 4 ½ fl. oz / ½ cup dark ale
1 litre / 1 pint 15 fl. oz / 4 cups vegetable stock
salt and pepper

METHOD

1. Put the butter in a slow cooker and cook on high until it melts. Stir in the onions, garlic, balsamic and honey and season well with salt and pepper. Cover and cook on high for 1 hour, stirring every 15 minutes.

2. Stir in the flour, then gradually incorporate the ale and stock, stirring constantly to remove any lumps. Cover and cook on low for 6 hours.

3. Taste the soup for seasoning and adjust with salt and pepper, then ladle into warm bowls and serve.

TOP TIP
Serve with bread topped with Gruyère and melted under a hot grill.

Curried Lentil Soup

SERVES 6

PREPARATION TIME 5 MINUTES

COOKING TIME 3 HOUR 10 MINUTES

INGREDIENTS

2 tbsp mustard oil, plus extra for drizzling
2 onions, finely chopped
2 cloves of garlic, crushed
2.5 cm (1 in) piece fresh root ginger, grated
1 tbsp curry powder
400 g / 14 oz / 3 ¼ cups red lentils
1.2 litres / 2 pints / 5 cups vegetable stock
coriander (cilantro) leaves to garnish
salt and pepper

METHOD

1. Heat the oil in a frying pan and fry the onion, garlic and ginger over a medium heat for 10 minutes to soften without colouring.

2. Stir in the curry powder and cook for 1 more minute, then scrape the contents of the pan into a slow cooker and stir in the lentils and stock.

3. Cover and cook on high for 3 hours or until the lentils are very soft. Transfer the soup to a liquidizer and blend until smooth, then season with salt and pepper.

4. Ladle the soup into warm bowls, then drizzle with mustard oil and garnish with coriander before serving.

TOP TIP
Try serving the soup with fresh naan bread for dunking.

Prawn and Noodle Broth

SERVES 4

PREPARATION TIME 15 MINUTES

COOKING TIME 2 HOUR 15 MINUTES

INGREDIENTS

300 g / 10 ½ oz / 2 cups raw king prawns
3 tbsp dried black Chinese mushrooms
2 tbsp Thai green curry paste
1 red chilli (chili), sliced
1 tbsp fish sauce
1 tsp caster (superfine) sugar
200 g / 7 oz / 1 ½ cups fresh egg noodles
100 g / 3 ½ oz / ¾ cup sugar snap peas

METHOD

1. Peel the prawns, leaving the tails intact, then put the heads and shells in a slow cooker with the mushrooms. Pour in 1 litre / 1 pint 15 fl. oz / 4 cups of water, then cover and cook on medium for 2 hours.

2. Strain the stock, then return it to the pan with the mushrooms, discarding the heads and shells.

3. Turn the heat to high and stir in the curry paste, chilli, fish sauce and caster sugar. Taste the broth and adjust with extra fish sauce or sugar accordingly.

4. Add the noodles and sugar snaps to the pan, then cover and cook for 5 minutes. Add the prawns, then cover and cook for 2 minutes or until they are just opaque. Ladle into bowls and serve.

TOP TIP

For a gluten-free alternative, replace the egg noodles with rice noodles.

SOUPS

Tomato and Leek Soup

SERVES 4

PREPARATION TIME 15 MINUTES

COOKING TIME 3 HOUR 30 MINUTES

INGREDIENTS

2 tbsp olive oil
2 leeks, finely chopped
2 cloves of garlic, crushed
1 tbsp concentrated tomato purée
400 g / 14 oz / 2 cups ripe tomatoes, chopped
1 litre / 1 pint 15 fl. oz / 4 cups vegetable stock
2 tbsp flat leaf parsley, chopped
salt and pepper

METHOD

1. Heat the oil in a slow cooker set to high.
   Reserve 2 tbsp of the leek for a garnish
   and stir the rest into the oil with the garlic.
   Season with salt and pepper, then cover
   and cook for 30 minutes, stirring every
   10 minutes.

2. Stir in the tomato purée, tomatoes and
   stock, then cover and cook on low for
   3 hours.

3. Transfer the soup to a liquidizer and
   blend until smooth, then pass through a
   sieve to remove any seeds and bits of skin.

4. Taste for seasoning, then ladle the soup
   into warm bowls. Mix the reserved leek
   with the parsley and sprinkle on top.

TOP TIP

Add 2 chopped red
peppers before cooking
for a more savoury
flavour.

Leek, Potato and Bacon Soup

SERVES 4

PREPARATION TIME 25 MINUTES

COOKING TIME 6 HOURS

INGREDIENTS

1 ham bone
2 leeks, finely chopped
450 g / 1 lb / 2 cups potatoes, peeled and cubed
2 cloves of garlic, crushed
8 rashers back bacon
100 ml / 3 ½ fl. oz / ½ cup double (heavy) cream
baby chard to garnish
salt and pepper

METHOD

1. Put the ham bone in a slow cooker and pour over enough cold water to cover. Cover and cook on low for 4 hours.

2. Remove and discard the bone, then stir in the leeks, potato and garlic. Cover and cook on medium for 2 hours.

3. Towards the end of the cooking time, grill the bacon for 2 minutes on each side or until crisp.

4. Transfer the soup to a liquidizer and blend until smooth. Season to taste with salt and pepper. Transfer 100 ml / 3 ½ fl. oz / ½ cup of the soup to a small measuring jug and add the cream. Use a stick blender held at a slight angle to aerate the mixture until it forms a creamy foam.

5. Pour the soup into warm bowls and spoon over the foam. Garnish with baby chard and black pepper and serve with the crispy bacon.

TOP TIP

Stir in ½ tsp of ground cumin at the end for a delicious savoury soup.

Japanese Prawn and Noodle Soup

SERVES 4

PREPARATION TIME 20 MINUTES

COOKING TIME 2 HOURS 10 MINUTES

INGREDIENTS

300 g / 10 ½ oz / 2 cups raw king prawns
15 g / ½ oz / ⅛ cup piece of kombu
4 tbsp dried bonito flakes
200 g / 7 oz / 2 cups fresh rice noodles
2 spring onions (scallions), thinly sliced
2 mild red chillies (chilies), thinly sliced
2 tbsp coriander (cilantro) leaves

METHOD

1. Peel the prawns and put the heads and shells in a slow cooker. Pour in 1 litre / 1 pint 15 fl. oz / 4 cups of water, then cover and cook on medium for 2 hours.

2. Stir in the kombu and bonito flakes, then cover and cook for 5 minutes.

3. Strain the stock, then return it to the pan and stir in the noodles and prawns. Cover and cook for 3 minutes or until the prawns just turn opaque.

4. Ladle the soup into warm bowls and serve garnished with spring onion, chilli and coriander.

TOP TIP
This soup is also delicious made with fresh egg noodles.

Fennel and Courgette Soup

SERVES 6

PREPARATION TIME **30 MINUTES**

COOKING TIME **4 HOURS**

INGREDIENTS

2 fennel bulbs, chopped with fronds reserved
2 courgettes (zucchinis), chopped
1 onion, finely chopped
2 cloves of garlic, finely chopped
1 tsp ground fennel seeds
1 litre / 1 pint 15 fl. oz / 4 cups vegetable stock
50 g / 1 ¾ oz / ½ cup Parmesan, grated
salt and pepper

METHOD

1. Mix the fennel with the courgette, onion, garlic and fennel seeds in a slow cooker, then pour over the stock.

2. Cover the slow cooker and cook on high for 4 hours. Transfer to a liquidizer and blend until smooth, then season to taste with salt and pepper.

3. Heat the oven to 180°C (160°C fan) / 350F / gas 4. Use a round cookie cutter to shape the Parmesan into 6 rounds on a non-stick baking tray.

4. Transfer the tray to the oven and cook for 3 minutes or until the cheese has melted. Leave to cool and harden on the tray for a few minutes, then lift with a palette knife.

5. Pour the soup into warm bowls and garnish with the reserved fennel fronds. Serve with the Parmesan crisps.

TOP TIP
This soup is also delicious served chilled and garnished with crumbled feta.

Creamy Cauliflower and Broccoli Soup

SERVES 4

PREPARATION TIME **15 MINUTES**

COOKING TIME **3 HOURS**

INGREDIENTS

1.2 litres / 2 pints / 4 ¾ cups vegetable stock
1 head of broccoli, chopped
1 cauliflower, chopped
1 bay leaf
150 ml / 5 ½ fl. oz / ⅔ cup double (heavy) cream
50 g / 1 ¾ oz / ½ cup piece of Parmesan
nutmeg for grating
salt and pepper

METHOD

1. Put the stock, broccoli, cauliflower and bay leaf in a slow cooker. Cover and cook on low for 3 hours.

2. Discard the bay leaf, then ladle the soup into a liquidizer and blend until smooth.

3. Stir in most the cream and season to taste with salt and pepper.

4. Pour the soup into warm bowls, drizzle over the remaining cream, then use a vegetable peeler to shave the Parmesan over the top. Finely grate a little nutmeg over the top and serve.

TOP TIP

Garnish with crumbled Stilton in place of the Parmesan.

Pumpkin and Rosemary Soup

SERVES 6

PREPARATION TIME **10 MINUTES**

COOKING TIME **4 HOURS**

INGREDIENTS

600 g / 1 lb 5 ½ oz / 3 cups pumpkin, peeled,
    deseeded and cut into chunks
1 onion, finely chopped
2 cloves of garlic, finely chopped
3 sprigs rosemary, plus extra to garnish
1 litre / 1 pint 15 fl. oz / 4 cups vegetable stock
2 slices stale crusty bread
salt and pepper

METHOD

1. Mix the pumpkin with the onion, garlic and
   rosemary in a slow cooker, then pour over
   the stock and season with salt and pepper.

2. Cover the slow cooker and cook on high for
   4 hours. Remove and discard the rosemary,
   then transfer the soup to a liquidizer and
   blend until smooth. Taste the soup and
   adjust the seasoning.

3. Pour the soup into warm bowls. Tear the
   bread into rough croutons and scatter on
   top, then garnish with fresh rosemary.

TOP TIP

This soup also works
really well with sweet
potato in place of
the pumpkin.

Pea and Ham Soup

SERVES **8**

PREPARATION TIME **5 MINUTES**

COOKING TIME **8 HOURS**

INGREDIENTS

ham hock

0 g / 14 oz / 3 ¼ cups green split peas

onion, finely chopped

cloves of garlic, crushed

bay leaf

lt and pepper

METHOD

1. Put all of the ingredients in a slow cooker and pour over 2 litres / 4 pints 2 fl. oz / 8 cups of water. Cover and cook on high for 8 hours.

2. Discard the bay leaf, then remove the ham hock from the soup and shred the meat off the bone.

3. Use an stick blender to purée most of the split peas, leaving some whole for texture. Stir in the shredded ham and taste for seasoning, then ladle into warm bowls and serve.

TOP TIP

Stir a handful of fresh peas through the soup 10 minutes before the end.

Main Meals

Bouillabaisse

SERVES 4

PREPARATION TIME 30 MINUTES

COOKING TIME 6 HOURS 10 MINUTES

INGREDIENTS

sea bass
gurnard
00 g / 10 ½ oz / 2 cups raw king prawns
langoustines
tbsp olive oil
onion, finely chopped
celery stick, finely chopped
carrot, finely chopped
cloves of garlic, crushed
tbsp Pernod
tomato, diced
pinch of saffron
50 g / 1 lb / 2 ¼ cups live mussels, scrubbed
tbsp flat leaf parsley, chopped
alt and pepper

METHOD

1. Fillet the fish and put the heads and bones in a slow cooker. Peel the prawns, keeping the tails intact, then add the heads to the slow cooker along with the langoustine heads.

2. Heat the oil in a frying pan and fry the onion, celery, carrot and garlic for 5 minutes without colouring.

3. Pour in the Pernod and bubble until almost evaporated, then scrape the contents of the pan into the slow cooker with the chopped tomato and saffron.

4. Add enough cold water to cover everything by 2.5 cm (1 in), then cover and cook on low for 6 hours.

5. Transfer the contents of the slow cooker to a liquidizer and blend until smooth, then pass the mixture through a sieve back into the slow cooker.

6. Cut the fish fillets into chunks and stir into the soup with the mussels, prawns and langoustines. Cover and cook on medium for 10 minutes or until the mussels open. Discard any that stay closed. Season to taste with salt and pepper, then ladle into bowls and serve garnished with parsley.

TOP TIP
Chill the soup overnight and reheat the next day.

Pot-roasted Guinea Fowl

SERVES **2**

PREPARATION TIME **15 MINUTES**

COOKING TIME **45 MINUTES**

INGREDIENTS

2 tbsp olive oil
2 guinea fowl leg quarters
1 leek, halved and sliced
1 carrot, diced
8 baby turnips, peeled
100 g / 3 ½ oz / 2 cups oyster mushrooms,
 torn into strips
2 sprigs fresh sage, plus extra to garnish
200 ml / 7 fl. oz / ¾ cup dry cider

METHOD

1. Preheat the oven to 180°C (160°C fan) / 350F / gas 4.

2. Heat the oil in a frying pan. Season the guinea fowl well with salt and pepper, then sear on all sides until browned.

3. Divide the leek, carrots, turnips, mushrooms and sage between two individual casserole dishes, then lay the guinea fowl legs on top.

4. Pour over the cider, then cover the dishes and bake them in the oven for 45 minutes. Insert a skewer into the thickest part of the thigh – if the juice runs clear, the meat is cooked.

5. Garnish the dishes with fresh sage and serve immediately.

TOP TIP
If you can't source guinea fowl, use chicken instead.

Stewed Peppers and Tomatoes

SERVES 4

PREPARATION TIME 5 MINUTES

COOKING TIME 2 HOURS 30 MINUTES

INGREDIENTS

3 tbsp olive oil
1 onion, sliced
2 red peppers, deseeded and cut into chunks
2 yellow peppers, deseeded and cut into chunks
2 green peppers, deseeded and cut into chunks
2 cloves of garlic, sliced
4 medium tomatoes
4 tbsp dry sherry
250 ml / 9 fl. oz / 1 cup vegetable stock
salt and pepper

METHOD

1. Put the oil in a slow cooker and heat on high. Stir in the onion and peppers and season with salt and pepper.

2. Cover and cook for 1 hour 30 minutes, stirring every 15 minutes.

3. Stir in the garlic, tomatoes and sherry, then pour over the vegetable stock.

4. Cover and cook on low for 2 hours, then season to taste before serving.

TOP TIP

Poach eggs directly into the stew, until the whites are cooked and the yolk runny.

Lamb, Courgette and Aubergine Tagine

SERVES **4**

PREPARATION TIME **10 MINUTES**

COOKING TIME **2 HOURS 15 MINUTES**

INGREDIENTS

450 g / 1 lb / 3 cups lamb shoulder, cubed

2 tsp ras el hanout spice mix

2 cinnamon sticks

2 tbsp olive oil

2 tbsp honey

1 onion, diced

1 courgette (zucchini), sliced

½ aubergine (eggplant), cut into chunks

1 red pepper, deseeded and cut into chunks

50 g / 1 ¾ oz / ¼ cup sultanas

250 ml / 9 fl. oz / 1 cup good quality lamb stock

2 tbsp flat leaf parsley, chopped

1 tbsp mint leaves, chopped

sea salt

METHOD

1. Preheat the oven to 160°C (140°C fan) / 325F / gas 3.

2. Put the lamb, spices, oil, honey, vegetables and sultanas in a large tagine with a big pinch of salt and stir well to mix.

3. Pour over the stock, then put on the lid and transfer the tagine to the oven. Cook the tagine for 2 hours.

4. Remove the lid, stir well and cook for another 15 minutes. Sprinkle with parsley and mint just before serving.

TOP TIP

For a more piquant taste, use capers instead of sultanas.

Salmon, Carrot and Olive Tagine

SERVES 4

PREPARATION TIME **10 MINUTES**

COOKING TIME **1 HOUR 30 MINUTES**

INGREDIENTS

3 carrots, peeled and sliced
2 tomatoes, halved
½ preserved lemon, sliced
1 onion, chopped
a pinch of saffron
250 ml / 9 fl. oz / 1 cup good quality fish stock
4 portions of salmon fillet
100 g / 3 ½ oz / ⅔ cup green olives
2 tbsp olive oil
1 tbsp flat leaf parsley, chopped

METHOD

1. Preheat the oven to 160°C (140°C fan) / 325F / gas 3.

2. Mix the carrots, tomatoes, preserved lemon and onion together in a tagine. Stir the saffron into the stock and pour it over the vegetables, then put on the lid and bake for 1 hour.

3. Arrange the salmon and olives on top of the vegetables and drizzle with the oil. Cover the tagine and return it to the oven, then turn the temperature down to 140°C (120°C fan) / 275F / gas 1.

4. Cook the tagine for another 30 minutes, then sprinkle with parsley and serve.

TOP TIP

This tagine also works really well with swordfish.

Squash and Chestnut Tagine

SERVES 4

PREPARATION TIME 10 MINUTES

COOKING TIME 3 HOURS

INGREDIENTS

1 butternut squash, peeled, deseeded and cut
   into chunks
12 chestnuts, peeled
8 pieces cassia bark
2.5 cm (1 in) piece root ginger, finely chopped
3 cloves of garlic, finely chopped
1 tsp ground cumin
1 tsp ground coriander (cilantro)
2 tbsp olive oil
400 ml / 14 fl. oz / 1 ²/₃ cups vegetable stock
coriander (cilantro) to garnish
salt and pepper

METHOD

1. Preheat the oven to 150°C (130°C fan)
   / 300F / gas 2.

2. Divide the squash and chestnuts between
   four individual tagines and top with the
   cassia bark. Stir the ginger, garlic, cumin,
   coriander and oil into the stock and season
   well with salt and pepper, then pour it over
   the vegetables.

3. Put the lids on the tagines and transfer
   them to the oven. Bake for 3 hours or until
   the squash and chestnuts are tender and
   garnish with coriander before serving.

TOP TIP

This recipe tastes
great made with sweet
potato too.

Chicken and Preserved Lemon Tagine

SERVES 4

PREPARATION TIME 15 MINUTES

COOKING TIME 2 HOURS

INGREDIENTS

2 tbsp olive oil
1 chicken, jointed
1 onion, diced
2 cloves of garlic, sliced
1 tsp ground coriander (cilantro)
1 tsp ground ginger
1 preserved lemon, sliced
100 g / 3 ½ oz / ⅔ cup kalamata olives
250 ml / 9 fl. oz / 1 cup chicken stock
coriander (cilantro) to garnish
sea salt

METHOD

1. Preheat the oven to 160°C (140°C fan) / 325F / gas 3.

2. Heat the oil in a frying pan and season the chicken with salt. Sear the chicken pieces on all sides, then transfer to a tagine.

3. Add the onion, garlic, spices, preserved lemon and olives to the tagine and mix well. Pour over the stock, then put on the lid and transfer the tagine to the oven.

4. Cook the tagine for 2 hours, then garnish with coriander and serve.

TOP TIP
Stir in a big handful of chopped flat leaf parsley at the end.

Braised Haricot Beans

SERVES 6

PREPARATION TIME 15 MINUTES

COOKING TIME 6–8 HOURS

INGREDIENTS

400 g / 14 oz / 2 ⅔ cups dried haricot beans,
    soaked overnight
1 onion, chopped
1 carrot, chopped
4 tomatoes, quartered
4 cloves of garlic, sliced
2 tbsp flat leaf parsley, chopped
salt and pepper

METHOD

1. Drain the beans from their soaking water and put them in a large saucepan of cold water. Bring to the boil and cook for 10 minutes, then drain well.

2. Mix the beans with the onion, carrot, tomatoes and garlic in a slow cooker. Pour over enough boiling water to cover everything by 5 cm (2 in), then cook on low for 6–8 hours or until the beans are tender, but still holding their shape.

3. Season the beans to taste with salt and pepper, then stir in the parsley and serve.

TOP TIP

Try using butterbeans or chickpeas in place of the haricot beans.

Veal Tagine with Pumpkin and Tomatoes

SERVES 4

PREPARATION TIME 20 MINUTES

COOKING TIME 3 HOURS

INGREDIENTS

450 g / 1 lb / 3 cups veal shoulder, cubed

2 tbsp plain (all-purpose) flour

2 tbsp olive oil

1 onion, finely chopped

4 cloves of garlic, crushed

2.5 cm (1 in) piece fresh root ginger, finely grated

50 g / 1 ¾ oz / ¼ cup sultanas

2 tsp ras el hanout spice mix

1 tbsp runny honey

1 tbsp coriander (cilantro), chopped, plus extra to garnish

250 ml / 9 fl. oz / 1 cup good quality veal stock

salt and pepper

For the pumpkin and tomato

400 g / 14 oz / 3 cups pumpkin, peeled and cubed

2 tbsp olive oil

2 tomatoes, sliced

½ lemon

2 tbsp runny honey

METHOD

1. Preheat the oven to 160°C (140°C fan) / 325F / gas 3.

2. Season the veal with salt and pepper and dust the pieces with flour to coat. Heat the oil in a large frying pan and sear the veal in batches on all sides.

3. Transfer the veal to a tagine and stir in the onion, garlic, ginger, sultanas, ras el hanout, honey and coriander. Season well with salt.

4. Pour over the stock, then put on the lid and transfer the tagine to the oven. Cook the tagine for 3 hours.

5. 1 hour before the end of the cooking time, put the pumpkin in a roasting tin, drizzle with oil and season with salt and pepper. Roast the pumpkin for 45 minutes, stirring half way through.

6. Add the tomatoes to the pan then squeeze over the lemon and drizzle with honey. Return to the oven for 15 minutes.

7. Taste the tagine and adjust the seasoning then divide between four individual serving tagines. Top with the pumpkin and tomato and garnish with coriander before serving.

TOP TIP
You can replace the veal with pork or turkey breast.

Rabbit, Carrot and Almond Tagine

SERVES 2

PREPARATION TIME 10 MINUTES

COOKING TIME 1 HOUR 45 MINUTES

INGREDIENTS

1 rabbit, jointed
4 baby carrots, halved lengthways
1 red onion, cut into wedges
3 cloves of garlic, finely chopped
2 slices preserved lemon
1 tsp ras el hanout spice mix
2 tbsp olive oil
2 tbsp runny honey
250 ml / 9 fl. oz / 1 cup chicken stock
2 tbsp flaked (slivered) almonds
1 tsp thyme leaves

METHOD

1. Preheat the oven to 160°C (140°C fan) / 325F / gas 3.

2. Divide the rabbit pieces, carrots, onion, garlic and preserved lemon between two individual tagines. Stir the ras el hanout, oil and honey into the stock and season with salt, then pour it over the rabbit.

3. Put the lids on the tagines and transfer them to the oven, then bake for 1 hour 30 minutes.

4. Remove the lids and sprinkle with almonds, then return to the oven for 15 minutes to brown the tops. Sprinkle with thyme and serve immediately.

TOP TIP

This tagine is also delicious made with whole quail.

Beef, Pepper and Olive Stew

SERVES **4**

PREPARATION TIME **15 MINUTES**

COOKING TIME **6 HOURS**

INGREDIENTS

450 g / 1 lb / 3 cups stewing beef, cubed
2 tbsp plain (all-purpose) flour
2 tbsp olive oil
1 red pepper, deseeded and cut into wedges
1 yellow pepper, deseeded and cut into wedges
1 green pepper, deseeded and cut into wedges
150 g / 5 ½ oz / 1 cup green olives, pitted
1 onion, finely chopped
3 cloves of garlic, crushed
2 tbsp concentrated tomato purée
2 bay leaves
a few sprigs of thyme
500 ml / 17 ½ fl. oz / 2 cups good quality
    beef stock
couscous to serve
salt and pepper

METHOD

1. Preheat the oven to 160°C (140°C fan) / 325F / gas 3.

2. Season the beef with salt and pepper and dust the pieces with flour to coat. Heat the oil in a large frying pan and sear the beef in batches on all sides.

3. Transfer the beef to a slow cooker and stir in the rest of the ingredients. Season well with salt and pepper.

4. Put the lid on the slow cooker and cook on low for 6 hours, stirring every 2 hours. Serve with couscous.

TOP TIP
You can also make this stew with lamb instead of beef.

Beef, Turnip and Lardon Stew

SERVES 4

PREPARATION TIME 20 MINUTES

COOKING TIME 6 HOURS

INGREDIENTS

450 g / 1 lb / 3 cups stewing beef, cubed
2 tbsp plain (all-purpose) flour
2 tbsp olive oil
100 g / 2 ⅓ oz / ½ cup lardons
6 small turnips, peeled and halved
125 ml / 4 ½ fl. oz / ½ cup red wine
1 onion, finely chopped
3 cloves of garlic, crushed
2 bay leaves
½ orange, zest pared into thin strips
500 ml / 17 ½ fl. oz / 2 cups good quality
    beef stock
salt and pepper

METHOD

1. Season the beef with salt and pepper and dust the pieces with flour to coat. Heat the oil in a large frying pan and sear the beef in batches on all sides.

2. Transfer the beef to a slow cooker, then fry the lardons and turnips until lightly coloured. Deglaze the pan with the wine, then tip everything into the slow cooker and stir in the rest of the ingredients. Season well with salt and pepper.

3. Put the lid on the slow cooker and cook on low for 6 hours, stirring every 2 hours.

TOP TIP

Try using stout instead of the red wine for a more savoury flavour.

Lamb Stew with Spring Vegetables

SERVES 4

PREPARATION TIME 20 MINUTES

COOKING TIME 5 HOURS 30 MINUTES

INGREDIENTS

- thick slices lamb neck, on the bone
- tbsp plain (all-purpose) flour
- tbsp olive oil
- 25 ml / 4 ½ fl. oz / ½ cup white wine
- 2 new potatoes, scrubbed
- leeks, cut into chunks
- 2 baby carrots, scrubbed
- 00 ml / 17 ½ fl. oz / 2 cups good quality
  lamb stock
- runner beans, halved and sliced lengthways
- tbsp kalamata olives
- at leaf parsley to garnish
- alt and pepper

METHOD

1. Preheat the oven to 160°C (140°C fan) / 325F / gas 3.

2. Season the lamb with salt and pepper and dust with flour to coat. Heat the oil in a large frying pan and sear the lamb on all sides.

3. Transfer the lamb to a slow cooker, then deglaze the pan with the wine and scrape it in with the lamb. Add the potatoes, leeks, carrots and stock to the slow cooker and season well with salt and pepper.

4. Put the lid on the slow cooker and cook on low for 5 hours. Stir in the beans and olives, then cover and cook for another 30 minutes. Serve garnished with parsley.

TOP TIP

You can also use oxtail in place of the lamb neck.

Braised Mince and Beans

SERVES *8*

PREPARATION TIME **15 MINUTES**

COOKING TIME *6–8 HOURS*

INGREDIENTS

2 tbsp olive oil
450 g / 1 lb / 3 cups minced beef
400 g / 14 oz / 2 ⅔ cups dried borlotti beans,
    soaked overnight
1 onion, finely chopped
4 cloves of garlic, crushed
1 carrot, finely chopped
4 tomatoes, finely chopped
2 tbsp concentrated tomato purée
salt and pepper

METHOD

1. Heat the oil in a frying pan and brown the mince.

2. Drain the beans from their soaking water and put them in a large saucepan of cold water. Bring to the boil and cook for 10 minutes, then drain well.

3. Mix everything together in a slow cooker, then pour over enough boiling water to cover everything by 5 cm (2 in). Cook on low for 6–8 hours or until the beans are tender, but still holding their shape.

4. Season the beans to taste with salt and pepper before serving.

TOP TIP

For a vegetarian alternative, use vegetarian mince.

Veal Blanquette

METHOD

1. Put everything except for the cream in a slow cooker and stir well to mix.

2. Cook on low for 4 hours. Stir in the cream and cook on high for 30 minutes.

3. Taste the sauce for seasoning and adjust with salt and black pepper.

SERVES 4

PREPARATION TIME 5 MINUTES

COOKING TIME 4 HOURS 30 MINUTES

INGREDIENTS

tbsp butter

00 g / 1 lb 12 oz / 4 cups veal shoulder, cubed

leek, sliced

carrot, chopped

celery stick, chopped

00 g / 7 oz / 1 ⅓ cups baby onions, peeled

50 g / 5 ½ oz / 1 cup baby button mushrooms

00 ml / 1 pint / 2 ½ cups light veal or chicken stock

00 ml / 10 ½ fl. oz / 1 ¼ cups double (heavy) cream

alt and pepper

TOP TIP

You can also use turkey or pork in place of the veal.

Lamb Chops with Tomato Sauce

SERVES 4

PREPARATION TIME 15 MINUTES

COOKING TIME 2 HOURS

INGREDIENTS

4 tbsp olive oil
8 lamb chops
4 rashers back bacon
2 bulbs of fennel, thickly sliced
1 onion, sliced
1 tbsp rosemary leaves
150 g / 5 ½ oz / 2 cups button mushrooms, sliced
100 ml / 3 ½ fl. oz / ½ cup dry white wine
400 ml / 7 fl. oz / 1 ⅔ cups tomato passata
a few sprigs of basil

METHOD

1. Heat the oil in a frying pan and sear the lamb chops on both sides, followed by the bacon. Transfer to a slow cooker and add the rest of the ingredients.

2. Cover and cook on high for 2 hours, then garnish with basil and serve.

TOP TIP
Try using pork chops in place of the lamb chops.

Prawn Bisque

SERVES 6

PREPARATION TIME **15 MINUTES**

COOKING TIME **3 HOURS 45 MINUTES**

INGREDIENTS

450 g / 1 lb / 3 cups small shell-on prawns (shrimps)

1 fennel bulb, diced

1 onion, diced

2 cloves of garlic, unpeeled

4 medium tomatoes, quartered

1 tbsp olive oil

1 tbsp brandy

1 litre / 1 pint 15 fl. oz / 4 cups fish stock

1 tbsp concentrated tomato purée

4 tbsp double (heavy) cream

9 large shell-on king prawns

salt and pepper

METHOD

1. Preheat the oven to 220°C (200°C fan) / 425F / gas 7.

2. Spread out the prawns, fennel, onion, garlic and tomatoes in a roasting tin. Drizzle with oil and season with salt and pepper, then roast for 15 minutes.

3. Stir the brandy into the roasting tin, then scrape everything into a slow cooker and stir in the fish stock and tomato purée. Cover and cook on medium for 3 hours.

4. Transfer the contents of the slow cooker to a liquidizer and blend until smooth.

5. Pass the bisque through a sieve back into the slow cooker. Stir in the cream and add the king prawns, then cover and cook on low for 30 minutes.

6. Taste the bisque and adjust the seasoning before serving.

TOP TIP

Use this method to make crab bisque too, but don't use the hard carapice.

Pork and Rosemary Stew

SERVES **4**

PREPARATION TIME **10 MINUTES**

COOKING TIME **4 HOURS 30 MINUTES**

INGREDIENTS

2 tbsp butter
800 g / 1 lb 12 oz / 5 ⅓ cups pork shoulder, cubed
1 onion, finely chopped
1 celery stick, finely chopped
4 medium potatoes, peeled and cubed
1 bay leaf
4 sprigs of rosemary
600 ml / 1 pint / 2 ½ cups chicken stock
300 ml / 10 ½ fl. oz / 1 ¼ cups double (heavy) cream
2 tsp grain mustard

METHOD

1. Heat the butter in a large frying pan and sear the pork on all sides. Transfer the pork to a slow cooker and stir in the rest of the ingredients, except for the cream and mustard.

2. Cover and cook on low for 4 hours.

3. Stir in the cream and mustard and cook on high for 30 minutes. Taste the sauce for seasoning and adjust with salt and black pepper.

TOP TIP

Add chopped green beans 15 minutes before the end of cooking.

Vegetable Tagine

SERVES 4

PREPARATION TIME 5 MINUTES

COOKING TIME 2 HOURS

INGREDIENTS

courgettes (zucchinis), cut into chunks
aubergine (eggplant), cut into chunks
red pepper, deseeded and cut into chunks
onion, finely chopped
cloves of garlic, finely chopped
400 g / 14 oz / 1 ¾ cups canned tomatoes,
   chopped
tsp ras el hanout spice mix
tbsp thyme leaves
salt and pepper

METHOD

1. Preheat the oven to 160°C (140°C fan) / 325F / gas 3.

2. Stir everything together in a large tagine with a big pinch of salt. Cover the tagine with its lid and transfer to the oven.

3. Cook the tagine for 2 hours, then taste and adjust the seasoning before serving.

TOP TIP
Try adding a handful of capers for a great piquant taste.

Mini Casseroles of Duck and Prawns

SERVES 4

PREPARATION TIME 5 MINUTES

COOKING TIME 1 HOUR

INGREDIENTS

1 duck breast, thinly sliced
16 raw king prawns, peeled
1 courgette (zucchini), diced
2.5 cm (1 in) piece fresh root ginger, julienned
1 clove of garlic, crushed
2 tbsp Shaoxing rice wine
2 tbsp light soy sauce
2 tsp runny honey
1 tbsp sesame seeds
1 tbsp coriander (cilantro), chopped

METHOD

1. Preheat the oven to 160°C (140°C fan) / 325F / gas 3.

2. Toss the duck with the prawns, courgette, ginger and garlic and divide between four mini casserole dishes. Stir the rice wine, so and honey together and drizzle over the top.

3. Put the lids on the casseroles, then transfe to the oven and bake for 1 hour.

4. Sprinkle with sesame seeds and coriander before serving.

TOP TIP
Try adding a chopped red pepper.

Pot au Feu

SERVES 4

PREPARATION TIME 20 MINUTES

COOKING TIME 8 HOURS

INGREDIENTS

450 g / 1 lb / 3 cups beef brisket
1 ham bone
8 small turnips, scrubbed
4 salad onions, peeled
4 carrots, peeled
3 cloves of garlic, sliced
2 bay leaves

METHOD

1. Put all of the ingredients in a slow cooker and pour over enough water to cover by 2.5 cm (1 in).

2. Cover and cook on low for 8 hours. Cut the beef into chunks or slices and serve with the vegetables and cooking liquor.

TOP TIP

Serve with plenty of crusty bread.

Pot-roasted Quail with Pears

SERVES 2

PREPARATION TIME 10 MINUTES

COOKING TIME 1 HOUR 30 MINUTES

INGREDIENTS

2 tbsp olive oil
2 oven-ready quail
2 pears, peeled and quartered
2 tsp mixed peppercorns
2 cloves
1 tbsp sultanas
1 lemon, juiced
1 tbsp runny honey

METHOD

1. Preheat the oven to 160°C (140°C fan) / 325F / gas 3.

2. Heat the oil in a frying pan and sear the quail on all sides.

3. Transfer the quail to a cast iron casserole dish and tuck the pear quarters around them. Sprinkle over the peppercorns, cloves and sultanas, then stir the lemon and honey together and drizzle over the top.

4. Put a lid on the dish and transfer to the oven, then cook for 1 hour. Remove the lid and cook for another 30 minutes.

TOP TIP
You can also use this method for cooking partridge when in season.

Chorizo, Potato and Sweetcorn Stew

SERVES 4

PREPARATION TIME 5 MINUTES

COOKING TIME 3 HOURS

INGREDIENTS

250 g / 9 oz / 1 ⅔ cups mini cooking chorizo

1 large potato, cut into wedges

2 corn cobs, cut into thick slices

4 spring onions (scallions), cut into short lengths

1 chipotle chilli (chili)

200 ml / 7 fl. oz / 1 ⅔ cups tomato passata

1 lime, cut into chunks

1 tbsp coriander (cilantro), chopped

METHOD

1. Mix all of the ingredients together, except for the lime and coriander, in a slow cooker.

2. Cover and cook on medium for 3 hours or until the potatoes are tender, but still holding their shape.

3. Spoon into warm bowls and garnish with lime chunks and coriander.

TOP TIP

This stew is also delicious with the addition of four sliced squid tubes.

Chorizo and Lentil Soup

SERVES 6

PREPARATION TIME 5 MINUTES

COOKING TIME 2 HOURS 30 MINUTES

INGREDIENTS

2 tbsp olive oil
225 g / 8 oz / 1 ½ cups chorizo ring, sliced
1 onion, finely chopped
1 celery stick, sliced
2 cloves of garlic, crushed
400 g / 14 oz / 3 ¼ cups red lentils
1.2 litres / 2 pint / 5 cups vegetable stock
1 bay leaf
6 cherry tomatoes, halved
salt and pepper

METHOD

1. Heat the oil in a large frying pan and fry the chorizo slices for 1 minute on each side. Transfer to a slow cooker and stir in the rest of the ingredients, except for the tomatoes.

2. Cover and cook on high for 2 hours, then stir in the tomatoes and cook for 30 minutes.

3. Taste the soup for seasoning and adjust with salt and pepper, then ladle into warm bowls and serve.

TOP TIP
You can also use green lentils to make this soup.

Chicken and Chickpea Tagine

SERVES 4

PREPARATION TIME **15 MINUTES**

COOKING TIME **2 HOURS**

INGREDIENTS

tbsp olive oil
chicken legs
leek, sliced
carrot, cut into chunks
courgette (zucchini), halved and sliced
50 g / 5 ½ oz / 1 cup canned chickpeas
red chilli (chili), deseeded and chopped
tsp ground cumin
tsp ground coriander (cilantro)
tsp ground ginger
tbsp coriander (cilantro) leaves
50 ml / 9 fl. oz / 1 cup chicken stock
sea salt

METHOD

1. Preheat the oven to 160°C (140°C fan) / 325F / gas 3.

2. Heat the oil in a frying pan and season the chicken with salt. Sear the chicken legs on all sides, then transfer to a tagine.

3. Mix in the rest of the ingredients, apart from the coriander, then put on the lid and transfer the tagine to the oven.

4. Cook the tagine for 2 hours, then garnish with coriander and serve.

TOP TIP
Try using butterbeans in place of the chickpeas.

Mussel and Cauliflower Stew

SERVES 6

PREPARATION TIME 5 MINUTES

COOKING TIME 2 HOURS 15 MINUTES

INGREDIENTS

1.2 litres / 2 pints / 4 ¾ cups fish stock
½ cauliflower, cut into florets
1 large potato, peeled and diced
1 celery stick, sliced
1 leek, sliced
2 bay leaves
2 tbsp flat leaf parsley, chopped
1.2 litres / 2 pints / 4 ¾ cups live mussels,
    scrubbed
salt and pepper

METHOD

1. Put the stock in a slow cooker with the vegetables, bay leaves and half of the parsley. Cover and cook on medium for 2 hours.

2. Stir the mussels into the pot, then cover and cook for 15 minutes or until they have all opened. Taste the soup and add salt and pepper as necessary, then sprinkle with parsley and serve.

TOP TIP

Try using clams or cockles instead of the mussels.

Lamb Meatball Tagine

SERVES 4

PREPARATION TIME 25 MINUTES

COOKING TIME 2 HOURS

INGREDIENTS

225 g / 8 oz / 1 cup minced lamb
225 g / 8 oz / 1 cup sausage meat
50 g / 2 oz / ²/₃ cup fresh white breadcrumbs
3 tbsp hummus
2 tbsp flat leaf parsley, finely chopped
2 tbsp olive oil
2 courgettes (zucchinis), cut into chunks
1 large potato, peeled and cut into chunks
1 carrot, peeled and sliced
1 onion, quartered and sliced
2 cloves of garlic, finely chopped
150 g / 5 ½ oz / 1 cup canned chickpeas
150 g / 5 ½ oz / 1 cup peas
200 g / 7 oz / 1 ⅓ cups cherry tomatoes
2 tsp ras el hanout spice mix
250 ml / 9 fl. oz / 1 cup lamb or vegetable stock
salt and pepper

METHOD

1. Knead the lamb mince, sausage meat, breadcrumbs, hummus and parsley together. Season with salt and pepper, then shape the mixture into meatballs.

2. Heat the oil in a frying pan and sear the meatballs on all sides.

3. Preheat the oven to 160°C (140°C fan) / 325F / gas 3.

4. Stir everything together in a large tagine with a big pinch of salt. Cover the tagine with its lid and transfer to the oven.

5. Cook the tagine for 2 hours, then taste and adjust the seasoning before serving.

TOP TIP
Try serving the tagine with hummus and flatbreads.

Pork and Flageolet Bean Stew

SERVES *8*

PREPARATION TIME *10 MINUTES*

COOKING TIME *6–8 HOURS*

INGREDIENTS

450 g / 1 lb / 3 cups pork shoulder,
    cut into chunks
400 g / 14 oz / 2 ⅔ cups dried flageolet beans,
    soaked overnight
1 onion, finely chopped
4 cloves of garlic, crushed
4 medium potatoes, quartered
2 carrots, cut into chunks
400 g / 14 oz / 1 ¾ cups canned tomatoes,
    chopped
100 g / 3 ½ oz / 2 cups baby leaf spinach
salt and pepper

METHOD

1. Drain the beans of their soaking liquid
   and put into the slow cooker with all the
   remaining ingredients, apart from the
   spinach. Add enough water to just cover
   everything.

2. Cover and cook on low for 6–8 hours or
   until the beans are tender, but still hold
   their shape.

3. Stir in the spinach, then cover and leave
   to stand for 5 minutes. Season to taste
   with salt and pepper before serving.

TOP TIP
You can also make this stew with veal instead of pork.

Lamb Chops with Apricots

METHOD

1. Heat the oil in a frying pan and season the lamb with salt and pepper. Sear the chops on both sides, then transfer to a slow cooker and add the rest of the ingredients apart from the sorrel.

2. Cover and cook on high for 2 hours, then garnish with sorrel and serve.

SERVES 4

PREPARATION TIME 15 MINUTES

COOKING TIME 2 HOURS

INGREDIENTS

4 tbsp olive oil
8 lamb chops
4 apricots, halved and stoned
4 cardamom pods
1 bay leaf
150 g / 5 ½ oz / 1 cup cherry tomatoes
100 ml / 3 ½ fl. oz / ½ cup dry white wine
400 ml / 7 fl. oz / 1 ⅔ cups tomato passata
2 tbsp sorrel leaves, shredded
salt and pepper

TOP TIP
This recipe is also delicious made with peaches or plums.

MAIN MEALS

Ham and Bean Soup

METHOD

1. Stir all of the ingredients together in a slow cooker, then cover and cook on medium for 6 hours.

2. Taste the soup for seasoning and adjust with salt and pepper, then ladle into warm bowls and serve.

SERVES 6

PREPARATION TIME 5 MINUTES

COOKING TIME 6 HOURS

INGREDIENTS

225 g / 8 oz / 1 ½ cups piece boiling ham, diced
1 onion, finely chopped
1 celery stick, sliced
1 carrot, chopped
2 cloves of garlic, crushed
1 medium tomato, diced
300 g / 10 ½ oz / 2 cups haricot beans, soaked
    overnight and drained
1.2 litres / 2 pint / 5 cups vegetable stock
1 bay leaf
salt and pepper

TOP TIP

Add a handful of fresh peas to the soup 10 minutes before the end of cooking.

Chicken, Potato and Pepper Tagine

SERVES 4

PREPARATION TIME 20 MINUTES

COOKING TIME 2 HOURS

INGREDIENTS

tbsp olive oil
chicken legs
onion, sliced
small potatoes, cut into wedges
red pepper, deseeded and diced
cloves of garlic, finely chopped
2.5 cm (1 in) piece fresh root ginger,
   finely chopped
tsp ground cumin
tsp ground coriander (cilantro)
tsp ground ginger
pinch of saffron
250 ml / 9 fl. oz / 1 cup chicken stock
sea salt

METHOD

1. Preheat the oven to 160°C (140°C fan) / 325F / gas 3.

2. Heat the oil in a large frying pan and season the chicken with salt. Sear the chicken legs on all sides, then transfer to a tagine.

3. Mix with in the rest of the ingredients, then put on the lid and transfer the tagine to the oven.

4. Cook the tagine for 2 hours, then leave to stand for 15 minutes before serving.

TOP TIP
Add a sliced chorizo to the tagine for a spicy kick.

Pot-roasted Chicken with Vegetables

METHOD

1. Preheat the oven to 180°C (160°C fan) / 350F / gas 4 and season the chicken all over with salt and pepper.

2. Heat the oil in a frying pan and sear the chicken on all sides.

3. Transfer the chicken to a large ovenproof saucepan or casserole dish and surround with the vegetables, rosemary and olives.

4. Pour over the wine, then cover the pan and transfer to the oven. Roast for 1 hour 30 minutes, then remove the lid and return to the oven for a further 30 minutes.

SERVES 4

PREPARATION TIME **15 MINUTES**

COOKING TIME **2 HOURS**

INGREDIENTS

1 oven-ready chicken
2 tbsp olive oil
1 red onion, thickly sliced
2 celery sticks, chopped
1 yellow pepper, deseeded and cut into chunks
2 tbsp rosemary
100 g / 3 ½ oz / ⅔ cup kalamata olives
700 ml / 1 pint 3 ½ fl. oz / 2 ¾ cups dry white wine
salt and pepper

TOP TIP
This method also works well with pheasant when in season.

Coq au Vin

EPARATION TIME 20 MINUTES

OKING TIME 5 HOURS

IGREDIENTS

small chicken legs
bsp plain (all-purpose) flour
sp mustard powder
bsp olive oil
bsp butter
0 g / 5 ½ oz / 1 cup pancetta, cubed
0 g / 7 oz / 1 ⅓ cups baby onions, peeled
ew sprigs of thyme
0 ml / 1 pint / 2 ½ cups red wine
0 g / 5 ½ oz / 2 cups button mushrooms, sliced
t leaf parsley to garnish
lt and pepper

METHOD

1. Season the chicken with salt and pepper, then toss with the flour and mustard powder to coat.

2. Heat half of the oil and butter in a sauté pan and sear the chicken pieces on all sides.

3. Remove the chicken from the pan and add the rest of the oil and butter, followed by the pancetta, onions and thyme. Sauté for 5 minutes, then pour in the wine and bring to a simmer.

4. Scrape the mixture into a slow cooker and add the seared chicken legs. Cover and cook on low for 4 hours, then stir in the mushrooms and cook for 1 more hour.

5. Taste and adjust the seasoning with salt and pepper, then serve garnished with the parsley.

TOP TIP

This recipe is also delicious made with guinea fowl or pheasant.

Pot-roasted Paupiettes of Veal

SERVES 4

PREPARATION TIME 25 MINUTES

COOKING TIME 1 HOUR

INGREDIENTS

4 good quality pork sausages, skinned
4 veal escalopes
2 tbsp olive oil
1 onion, sliced
2 carrots, sliced
a few sprigs of thyme
200 g / 7 oz / ¾ cup canned tomatoes, chopped
150 ml / 5 ½ fl. oz / ⅔ cup dry white wine
salt and pepper

METHOD

1. Preheat the oven to 180°C (160°C fan) / 350F / gas 4.

2. Put a quarter of the sausage meat on top of each escalope, then gather up the sides into a ball and tie securely with string.

3. Heat the oil in a frying pan and sear the paupiettes on all sides.

4. Transfer the paupiettes to a cast iron casserole dish and surround with the onion, carrots and thyme. Stir the tomatoes into the wine, then pour it over the top.

5. Cover the pan and cook in the oven for 1 hour. Season the vegetables to taste with salt and pepper just before serving.

TOP TIP

This recipe can also be made with turkey or pork escalopes.

Beef in Red Wine with Shallots

SERVES 4

PREPARATION TIME 20 MINUTES

COOKING TIME 6 HOURS

INGREDIENTS

450 g / 1 lb / 3 cups chuck steak, cut into
    large chunks
1 tbsp plain (all-purpose) flour
1 tbsp olive oil
8 large shallots, halved
500 ml / 17 ½ fl. oz / 2 cups red wine
2 bay leaves
flat leaf parsley to garnish
mashed potato to serve
salt and pepper

METHOD

1. Season the beef with salt and pepper and dust the pieces with flour to coat. Heat the oil in a large frying pan and sear the beef in batches on all sides. Remove the beef from the pan, then colour the cut side of the shallots.

2. Transfer the beef and shallots to a slow cooker, tuck in the bay leaves and pour over the wine. Season well with salt and pepper.

3. Put the lid on the slow cooker and cook on low for 6 hours, stirring every 2 hours. Garnish with parsley and serve with mashed potato.

TOP TIP

Try using white wine for a lighter stew.

Pot-roasted Rabbit

SERVES 4

PREPARATION TIME 15 MINUTES

COOKING TIME 1 HOUR

INGREDIENTS

1 rabbit, jointed
1 tbsp plain (all-purpose) flour
2 tbsp olive oil
1 onion, sliced
2 carrots, sliced
1 tbsp sage leaves, chopped, plus extra
    to garnish
150 ml / 5 ½ fl. oz / ⅔ cup dry white wine
150 ml / 5 ½ fl. oz / ⅔ cup chicken stock
salt and pepper

METHOD

1. Preheat the oven to 180°C (160°C fan) / 350F / gas 4.

2. Season the rabbit well with salt and pepper, then dust with flour to coat.

3. Heat the oil in a frying pan and sear the rabbit on all sides.

4. Transfer to a cast iron casserole dish and surround with the onion, carrots and sage. Stir the stock and wine together, then pour it over the top.

5. Cover the pan and cook in the oven for 1 hour. Season to taste with salt and pepper, then serve, garnished with sage.

TOP TIP

Try replacing half of the carrots with parsnips.

Les Confitures Extra
de
Christine Ferber

Framboises et viole...

Preserves

Apple, Pear and Rhubarb Compote

METHOD

1. Mix all of the ingredients together in a slow cooker, then put on the lid and cook on low for 2 hours.

2. Puree the compote with a liquidizer and serve warm or chilled.

SERVES 6

PREPARATION TIME 10 MINUTES

COOKING TIME 2 HOURS

INGREDIENTS

4 rhubarb stalks, chopped
2 Bramley apples, peeled, cored and diced
6 pears, peeled, cored and diced
6 tbsp caster (superfine) sugar

TOP TIP
This makes a great accompaniment to grilled mackerel.

Blackberry and Raspberry Jam

MAKES 3 X 450 G JARS

PREPARATION TIME 5 MINUTES

COOKING TIME 4–5 HOURS

INGREDIENTS

500 g / 1 lb 2 oz / 3 ½ cups raspberries
500 g / 1 lb 2 oz / 3 ½ cups blackberries
900 g / 2 lb / 4 cups preserving sugar
50 g / 1 ¾ oz / ¼ cup powdered pectin
2 tbsp lemon juice

METHOD

1. Stir all of the ingredients together in a large slow cooker.

2. Cook on low for 2 hours, stirring well halfway through.

3. Put a saucer in the freezer. Increase the heat to high and cook for 2 hours. To test if the jam is ready, spoon a small amount onto the frozen saucer. Wait a few seconds, then push the side of the jam with a spoon. If the surface wrinkles, it is ready. If not, continue to cook on high and check again every 30 minutes.

4. Ladle the hot jam into sterilized jars and screw the lids on securely.

TOP TIP
Try using the jam as the filling for a sponge cake.

Apricot, Almond and Pistachio Jam

MAKES 3 X 450 G JARS

PREPARATION TIME 5 MINUTES

COOKING TIME 4–5 HOURS

INGREDIENTS

1 kg / 2 lb 3 oz / 5 ½ cups apricots, quartered
    and stoned
900 g / 2 lb / 4 cups preserving sugar
50 g / 1 ¾ oz / ¼ cup powdered pectin
100 g / 2 ⅓ oz / 1 ⅓ cups flaked (slivered) almonds
100 g / 3 ½ oz / ¾ cup slivered pistachio nuts

METHOD

1. Stir the apricots, sugar and pectin together in a large slow cooker.

2. Cook on low for 2 hours, stirring well halfway through.

3. Put a saucer in the freezer. Increase the heat to high and cook for 2 hours. To test if the jam is ready, spoon a small amount onto the frozen saucer. Wait a few seconds, then push the side of the jam with a spoon. If the surface wrinkles, it is ready. If not, continue to cook on high and check again every 30 minutes.

4. Stir the almonds and pistachio nuts into the jam, then ladle it into sterilized jars and screw the lids on securely.

TOP TIP

This jam makes a great filling for a Bakewell tart.

Strawberry Jam

MAKES 3 X 450 G JARS

PREPARATION TIME 5 MINUTES

COOKING TIME 4–5 HOURS

INGREDIENTS

1 kg / 2 lb 3 oz / 7 cups strawberries, sliced
900 g / 2 lb / 4 cups preserving sugar
60 g / 1 ¾ oz / ¼ cup powdered pectin
2 lemons, juiced

METHOD

1. Stir all of the ingredients together in a large slow cooker.

2. Cook on low for 2 hours, stirring well halfway through.

3. Put a saucer in the freezer. Increase the heat to high and cook for 2 hours. To test if the jam is ready, spoon a small amount onto the frozen saucer. Wait a few seconds, then push the side of the jam with a spoon. If the surface wrinkles, it is ready. If not, continue to cook on high and check again every 30 minutes.

4. Ladle the hot jam into sterilized jars and screw the lids on securely.

TOP TIP
Try adding the seeds from two vanilla pods just before decanting into jars.

Blackberry Jelly

MAKES 500 ML

PREPARATION TIME 15 MINUTES

COOKING TIME 20 MINUTES

INGREDIENTS

450 g / 1 lb / 2 cups granulated sugar
450 g / 1 lb / 3 cups blackberries
2 lemons, juiced

METHOD

1. Preheat the oven to 110°C (90° fan) / 225F / gas ¼.

2. Put the sugar in a heatproof bowl and transfer it to the oven along with 2 small glass jars.

3. Put the blackberries and lemon juice in a large saucepan and cover with a lid. Heat gently for 10 minutes or until the blackberries have burst and cooked down into a purée.

4. Stir in the warmed sugar to dissolve then increase the heat and boil for 8 minutes.

5. Pour the mixture into a muslin-lined colander set over a bowl to strain out the seeds.

6. Ladle the jelly into the prepared jars while it's still hot, then seal with clean lids or waxed paper.

TOP TIP

For a better set, add 1 finely chopped Bramley apple before cooking.

Les Confitures Extra
de
Christine Ferber
Framboises et violet

Raspberry and Violet Conserve

MAKES 4 X 450 G JARS

PREPARATION TIME 5 MINUTES

COOKING TIME 4–5 HOURS

INGREDIENTS

2 kg / 4 lb 6 oz / 14 cups raspberries
900 g / 2 lb / 4 cups preserving sugar
50 g / 1 ¾ oz / ¼ cup powdered pectin
75 ml / 2 ½ fl. oz / ⅓ cup violet syrup

METHOD

1. Stir the raspberries, sugar and pectin together in a large slow cooker.

2. Cook on low for 2 hours, stirring well half way through. Pass the mixture through a sieve to remove the seeds and wash and dry the slow cooker.

3. Put a saucer in the freezer, then return the purée to the slow cooker and increase the heat to high and cook for 2 hours. To test if the mixture is ready, spoon a small amount onto the frozen saucer. If it is just thick enough to spread, it is ready. If it is too runny, continue to cook on high and check again every 30 minutes.

4. When you are happy with the consistency, stir in the violet syrup, then ladle the hot conserve into sterilized jars and screw the lids on securely. The high fruit content of this conserve means it should be stored in the fridge and has a shorter shelf life than other jams.

TOP TIP
This delicate conserve is a great afternoon tea treat.

Lemon and Lime Marmalade

MAKES 3 X 450 G JARS

PREPARATION TIME 15 MINUTES

COOKING TIME 6–7 HOURS

INGREDIENTS

2 unwaxed lemons, quartered and pips removed
4 unwaxed limes, quartered
900 g / 2 lb / 4 cups preserving sugar

METHOD

1. Put the lemons and limes into a slow cooker and pour in 1.2 litres / 2 pints / 5 cups of water. Cook on low for 4 hours.

2. Transfer the contents of the slow cooker to a liquidizer and pulse until the fruit is finely chopped. Return the pulp to the pan and stir in the sugar until dissolved.

3. Put a saucer in the freezer. Increase the heat to high and cook for 2 hours. To test if the marmalade is ready, spoon a small amount onto the frozen saucer. Wait a few seconds, then push the side of the marmalade with a spoon. If the surface wrinkles, it is ready. If not, continue to cook on high and check every 30 minutes.

4. Ladle the hot marmalade into sterilized jars and screw the lids on securely.

TOP TIP
Try using the marmalade as an usual filling for a Victoria sponge.

Raspberry Jam

MAKES 3 X 450 G JARS

PREPARATION TIME 5 MINUTES

COOKING TIME 4–5 HOURS

INGREDIENTS

1 kg / 2 lb 3 oz / 7 cups raspberries
900 g / 2 lb / 4 cups preserving sugar
30 g / 1 ¾ oz / ¼ cup powdered pectin
2 tbsp lemon juice

METHOD

1. Stir all of the ingredients together in a large slow cooker.

2. Cook on low for 2 hours, stirring well halfway through.

3. Put a saucer in the freezer. Increase the heat to high and cook for 2 hours. To test if the jam is ready, spoon a small amount onto the frozen saucer. Wait a few seconds, then push the side of the jam with a spoon. If the surface wrinkles, it is ready. If not, continue to cook on high and check again every 30 minutes.

4. Ladle the hot jam into sterilized jars and screw the lids on securely.

TOP TIP
Serve the jam with fresh scones and clotted cream.

PRESERVES

Exotic Fruit Compote

SERVES 6

PREPARATION TIME **10 MINUTES**

COOKING TIME **1 HOUR 30 MINUTES**

INGREDIENTS

3 mangoes, peeled, stoned and diced
2 papayas, peeled, deseeded and diced
6 passion fruit, halved
2 limes, juiced
4 tbsp caster (superfine) sugar
2 tbsp coconut rum

METHOD

1. Put the mango and papaya in a slow cooker and scoop in the passion fruit seeds and flesh. Stir in the lime juice, sugar and coconut rum.

2. Put on the lid and cook on low for 1 hour 30 minutes or until the fruit has started to break down. Leave the compote chunky or use a stick blender to purée the fruit and serve hot or chilled.

TOP TIP

Try serving the compote with coconut ice cream.

Apple Compote

METHOD

1. Mix all of the ingredients together in a slow cooker, then put on the lid and cook on low for 2 hours.

2. Purée the compote with a liquidizer and serve warm or chilled.

SERVES 6

PREPARATION TIME 5 MINUTES

COOKING TIME 2 HOURS

INGREDIENTS

Bramley apples, peeled, cored and diced

eating apples, peeled, cored and diced

lemon, juiced

50 ml / 5 ½ fl. oz / ²/₃ cup apple juice

tbsp caster (superfine) sugar

TOP TIP

This makes a delicious accompaniment to roast pork or duck.

Fig and Pine Nut Conserve

METHOD

1. Stir the figs, lemon juice, sugar and pectin together in a large slow cooker.

2. Cook on low for 2 hours, stirring well halfway through. Use a food processor to purée the fruit and wash and dry the slow cooker.

3. Put a saucer in the freezer, then return the purée to the slow cooker and increase the heat to high and cook for 2 hours. To test if the conserve is ready, spoon a small amount onto the frozen saucer. If it is just thick enough to spread, it is ready. If it is too runny, continue to cook on high and check again every 30 minutes.

4. When you are happy with the consistency, stir in the pine nuts, then ladle the hot confiture into sterilized jars and screw the lids on securely. The high fruit content of this conserve means it should be stored in the fridge and has a shorter shelf life than other jams.

MAKES 4 X 450 G JARS

PREPARATION TIME 5 MINUTES

COOKING TIME 4–5 HOURS

INGREDIENTS

2 kg / 4 lb 6 oz / 10 cups ripe figs, diced
2 lemons, juiced
900 g / 2 lb / 4 cups preserving sugar
50 g / 1 ¾ oz / ¼ cup powdered pectin
150 g / 5 ½ oz / 1 cup pine nuts

TOP TIP
Serve the confiture with mature cheeses.

Peach Jam

MAKES 3 X 450 G JARS

PREPARATION TIME 5 MINUTES

COOKING TIME 4–5 HOURS

INGREDIENTS

1 kg / 2 lb 3 oz / 5 ½ cups peaches stoned
and chopped
900 g / 2 lb / 4 cups preserving sugar
50 g / 1 ¾ oz / ¼ cup powdered pectin

METHOD

1. Stir the peaches, sugar and pectin together in a large slow cooker.

2. Cook on low for 2 hours, stirring well halfway through.

3. Put a saucer in the freezer. Increase the heat to high and cook for 2 hours. To test if the jam is ready, spoon a small amount onto the frozen saucer. Wait a few seconds, then push the side of the jam with a spoon. If the surface wrinkles, it is ready. If not, continue to cook on high and check again every 30 minutes.

4. Ladle the hot jam into sterilized jars and screw the lids on securely.

TOP TIP

This jam is delicious served with fresh crêpes and vanilla ice cream.

Apple and Raspberry Compote

SERVES 6

PREPARATION TIME 5 MINUTES

COOKING TIME 2 HOURS

INGREDIENTS

2 Bramley apples, peeled, cored and diced
6 eating apples, peeled, cored and diced
200 g / 7 oz / 1 ⅓ cups raspberries
150 ml / 5 ½ fl. oz / ⅔ cup apple juice
4 tbsp caster (superfine) sugar

METHOD

1. Mix all of the ingredients together in a slow cooker, then put on the lid and cook on low for 2 hours.

2. Pass the compote through a sieve to purée the apples and remove the raspberry seeds. Taste the compote and add a little more sugar if it is too sharp.

TOP TIP

Serve the compote for breakfast with thick Greek yogurt and granola.

Pear Compote

METHOD

1. Mix all of the ingredients together in a slow cooker, then put on the lid and cook on low for 2 hours.

2. Puree the compote with a liquidizer and serve warm or chilled.

SERVES 6

PREPARATION TIME 5 MINUTES

COOKING TIME 2 HOURS

INGREDIENTS

Bramley apples, peeled, cored and diced

pears, peeled, cored and diced

lemons, juiced

tbsp caster (superfine) sugar

TOP TIP

This makes a delicious accompaniment to roast game dishes.

Cranberry Sauce

METHOD

1. Stir the cranberries, sugar and orange juice together in a small slow cooker.

2. Cover and cook on high for 2 hours or until the cranberries have burst and softened.

3. Ladle the sauce into a sterilized jar and leave to cool completely before storing in the fridge.

MAKES 1 X 450 G JARS

PREPARATION TIME 10 MINUTES

COOKING TIME 2 HOURS

INGREDIENTS

450 g / 1 lb / 2 ½ cups cranberries
200 g / 7 oz / ¾ cup caster (superfine) sugar
1 orange, juiced

TOP TIP
Add a finely chopped red chilli (chili) for a spicy kick.

Cinnamon Apple Compote

METHOD

1. Mix all of the ingredients together in a slow cooker, then put on the lid and cook on low for 2 hours.

2. Spoon the compote into sterilized jars and seal whilst still hot.

MAKES 2 X 450 G JARS

PREPARATION TIME 5 MINUTES

COOKING TIME 2 HOURS

INGREDIENTS

2 Bramley apples, peeled, cored and diced
8 eating apples, peeled, cored and diced
1 lemon, juiced
150 ml / 5 ½ fl. oz / ⅔ cup apple juice
4 tbsp caster (superfine) sugar
2 cinnamon sticks

TOP TIP
Use the compote as the filling to mini apple pies.

Poached Rhubarb in Chocolate Cases

SERVES 6

PREPARATION TIME **45 MINUTES**

COOKING TIME **2 HOURS**

INGREDIENTS

800 g / 1 lb 12 ½ oz / 5 cups rhubarb stalks
150 g / 5 ½ oz / ⅔ cup caster (superfine) sugar
50 g / 1 ¾ oz / ⅓ cup white chocolate
150 g / 5 ½ oz / 1 cup milk chocolate

METHOD

1. Cut the rhubarb into short lengths and put it in a slow cooker. Sprinkle over the sugar and 3 tbsp of water, then cover and cook on medium for 2 hours. Leave to cool, then chill in the fridge.

2. To make the chocolate cases, line six tartlet cases with cling film. Melt the white chocolate in a microwave or bain-marie, then drizzle it into the cases. Chill in the fridge for 15 minutes to set.

3. Melt the milk chocolate, then spoon it into the tartlet cases and tilt to coat in a thin, even layer. Turn the moulds upside down onto a tray and return to the fridge for 20 minutes.

4. Unmould the chocolate cases and remove the cling film, then spoon in the rhubarb compote to serve.

TOP TIP
Try serving the desserts with stem ginger ice cream.

Spiced Plum Compote

METHOD

1. Put the spices in a small square of muslin and tie into a bag with string. Put the spice bag in a slow cooker with the plums and sugar and drizzle over 3 tbsp of water.

2. Cover and cook on medium for 2 hours. Taste for sweetness and add extra sugar if necessary. Discard the spice bag and serve warm or cold.

SERVES 6

PREPARATION TIME 5 MINUTES

COOKING TIME 2 HOURS

INGREDIENTS

1 star anise

1 cinnamon stick, broken into pieces

4 cloves

16 plums, peeled, stoned and chopped

4 tbsp caster (superfine) sugar

TOP TIP

Try serving this compote with fresh crêpes and vanilla ice cream.

Desserts

DESSERTS

Chocolate Rice Pudding

SERVES 5

PREPARATION TIME 15 MINUTES

COOKING TIME 3 HOURS

INGREDIENTS

50 g / 1 ¾ oz / ¼ cup butter, plus extra for
    greasing
1.2 litres / 2 pints / 4 ½ cups whole milk
3 tbsp unsweetened cocoa powder
110 g / 4 oz / ½ cup short-grain rice
75 g / 2 ½ oz / ⅓ cup caster (superfine) sugar
100 g / 3 ½ oz / ⅔ cup dark chocolate (minimum
    70% cocoa solids)
4 tbsp clotted cream

METHOD

1. Butter the inside of a slow cooker. Stir all
   of the ingredients together except for the
   chocolate and cream, then tip the mixture
   into the slow cooker.

2. Cover and cook on high for 3 hours, stirring
   once every hour.

3. Break the chocolate into small squares,
   then remove the inner pan from the slow
   cooker and distribute the chocolate over
   the surface of the rice pudding. Cover and
   leave to stand for 5 minutes, then gently
   stir everything together.

4. Serve warm or chilled, topped with a
   spoonful of clotted cream.

TOP TIP
Add zest of an orange
and a pinch of Cayenne
pepper before cooking.

Chocolate Fondue

SERVES 6–8

PREPARATION TIME **5 MINUTES**

COOKING TIME **30 MINUTES**

INGREDIENTS

200 g / 7 oz / 1 ⅓ cups dark chocolate (minimum 70% cocoa solids)
300 ml / 10 ½ fl. oz / 1 ¼ cups double (heavy) cream
1 tbsp butter
1 tbsp runny honey
1 tbsp brandy
small sponge cakes to serve

METHOD

1. Break the chocolate into small squares and mix it with the cream, butter, honey and brandy in a small slow cooker.

2. Cover and cook on low for 30 minutes or until the chocolate has melted and combined with the cream, stirring every 10 minutes.

3. Serve the fondue in the slow cooker at the table to keep it warm or transfer to a serving bowl. Thread small sponge cakes onto skewers for your guests to dip in.

TOP TIP
Add the grated zest of an orange and a pinch of Cayenne pepper for added zing.

Pears in Red Wine with Thyme

SERVES 4

PREPARATION TIME 5 MINUTES

COOKING TIME 2 HOURS

INGREDIENTS

8 small pears, peeled and cored, stalks left intact
2 tbsp caster (superfine) sugar
500 ml / 17 ½ fl. oz / 2 cups red wine
3 sprigs of thyme

METHOD

1. Put everything in a slow cooker, then cover and cook on medium for 2 hours, turning th pears half way through.

2. Serve warm or chilled.

TOP TIP
You could also use rosemary instead of thyme.

Orange and Ginger Bundt Cake

SERVES 8

PREPARATION TIME **15 MINUTES**

COOKING TIME **3 HOURS**

INGREDIENTS

225 g / 8 oz / 1 ½ cups self-raising flour
100 g / 3 ½ oz / ½ cup butter, cubed
100 g / 3 ½ oz / ½ cup caster (superfine) sugar
2 tsp ground ginger
1 large egg
75 ml / 2 ½ fl. oz / ⅓ cup whole milk
1 orange, juiced and zest finely grated

METHOD

1. Put a rack in the bottom of a slow cooker and add 2.5 cm (1 in) of boiling water, then butter a bundt tin that will fit inside your slow cooker.

2. Sieve the flour into a mixing bowl and rub in the butter until it resembles fine breadcrumbs, then stir in the sugar and ground ginger.

3. Lightly beat the egg with the milk, orange juice and zest and stir it into the dry ingredients until just combined.

4. Scrape the mixture into the tin, then transfer it to the slow cooker. Cook on high for 3 hours or until a skewer inserted in the centre comes out clean. Transfer the cake to a wire rack and leave to cool completely.

TOP TIP

Drizzle with dark chocolate and sprinkle with crystalized ginger pieces.

DESSERTS

Chunky Pear and Vanilla Compote

METHOD

1. Mix all of the ingredients together, apart from the ice cream, in a slow cooker, then put on the lid and cook on low for 2 hours.

2. Leave the compote to cool to room temperature, then chill in the fridge. Serve with scoops of vanilla ice cream.

SERVES 6

PREPARATION TIME 5 MINUTES

COOKING TIME 2 HOURS

INGREDIENTS

2 Bramley apples, peeled, cored and diced
8 pears, peeled, cored and diced
1 lemon, juiced
4 tbsp caster (superfine) sugar
1 vanilla pod, split lengthways
vanilla ice cream to serve

TOP TIP
Use the compote as a base for crumbles or pies.

Poached Peaches with Lavender

SERVES 4

PREPARATION TIME **30 MINUTES**

COOKING TIME **1 HOUR 30 MINUTES**

INGREDIENTS

6 peaches, halved and stoned
100 g / 3 ½ oz / ½ cup caster (superfine) sugar
2 sprigs lavender

METHOD

1. Put the peaches in a slow cooker with the sugar and lavender and pour over 200 ml / 7 fl. oz / ¾ cup of water.

2. Cover and cook on medium for 1 hour 30 minutes or until the fruit is tender, but still holding its shape.

3. Peel off and discard the peach skins and lavender stems before serving.

TOP TIP

This recipe also works really well with plums.

Vanilla Poached Cherries

SERVES 6

PREPARATION TIME **10 MINUTES**

COOKING TIME **1 HOUR 30 MINUTES**

INGREDIENTS

900 g / 2 lb / 5 cups black cherries, stoned
100 g / 3 ½ oz / ½ cup caster (superfine) sugar
100 ml / 3 ½ fl. oz / ½ cup rosé wine
1 vanilla pod, split lengthways
3 tbsp kirsch
vanilla ice cream to serve

METHOD

1. Mix the cherries with the sugar, wine and vanilla pod in a slow cooker. Cover and cook on medium for 1 hour 30 minutes, then stir in the kirsch and leave to cool.

2. Discard the vanilla pod, then spoon the cherries and their cooking liquor into bowls and serve with vanilla ice cream.

TOP TIP

You can also use mirabelles or small greengages in place of the cherries.

Chocolate Muffin Puddings

SERVES 6

PREPARATION TIME 20 MINUTES

COOKING TIME 2 HOURS

INGREDIENTS

1 large egg
125 ml / 4 ½ fl. oz / ½ cup sunflower oil
125 ml / 4 ½ fl. oz / ½ cup milk
350 g / 12 ½ oz / 2 ⅓ cups self-raising flour, sifted
50 g / 1 ¾ oz / ½ cup unsweetened cocoa
    powder, sifted
1 tsp baking powder
200 g / 7 oz / ¾ cup caster (superfine) sugar
3 sugar cubes

METHOD

1. Put a rack inside a slow cooker and add 2.5 cm (1 in) of boiling water, then set it to high. Butter six mini casserole dishes or pudding basins.

2. Beat the egg in a jug with the oil and milk until well mixed. Mix the flour, cocoa, baking powder and caster sugar in a bowl, then pour in the egg mixture and stir just enough to combine.

3. Divide the mixture between the dishes and transfer to the slow cooker. Lay three layers of kitchen paper over the top of the slow cooker before putting on the lid to absorb the condensing steam.

4. Cook the puddings on high for 2 hours. Crumble over the sugar cubes and serve warm.

TOP TIP
Serve with fresh cream or vanilla ice cream as a treat.

Blueberry and Raspberry Bread and Butter Pudding

SERVES 4–6

PREPARATION TIME **10 MINUTES**

COOKING TIME **1 HOUR 30 MINUTES**

INGREDIENTS

8 slices white bread
4 tbsp butter, softened
100 g / 3 ½ oz / ⅔ cup blueberries
50 g / 1 ¾ oz / ⅓ cup raspberries
250 ml / 9 fl. oz / 1 cup milk
200 ml / 7 fl. oz / ¾ cup double (heavy) cream
4 large egg yolks
75 g / 2 ½ oz / ⅓ cup caster (superfine) sugar
1 lemon, zest finely grated
demerara sugar for sprinkling

METHOD

1. Spread the bread with butter, then cut each slice into squares and toss with the blueberries and raspberries in a large baking dish.

2. Whisk the milk, cream, eggs, sugar and lemon zest together and pour it over the bread, then leave to soak for 10 minutes.

3. Preheat the oven to 150°C (130°C fan) / 300F / gas 2. Bake the pudding for 1 hour 30 minutes or until the custard is just set with a slight wobble in the centre.

4. Sprinkle with demerara sugar and serve.

TOP TIP
You can also use stoned cherries instead of the blueberries and raspberries.

DESSERTS

Chocolate and Cherry Summer Pudding

SERVES 8

PREPARATION TIME 45 MINUTES

COOKING TIME 2 HOURS

CHILLING TIME 4 HOURS

INGREDIENTS

450 g / 1 lb / 3 cups cherries, stoned and halved

4 tbsp caster (superfine) sugar

4 tbsp kirsch

6 slices white bread, crusts removed

250 ml / 9 fl. oz / 1 cup double (heavy) cream

250 g / 9 oz / 1 ⅔ cups dark chocolate (minimum 60 % cocoa solids), chopped

METHOD

1. Stir the cherries, sugar and kirsch into a small slow cooker. Cover and cook on low for 2 hours, stirring half way through. Leave to cool, then strain the cherries through a sieve and collect the juice.

2. Line a pudding basin with cling film. Dip the bread in the cherry juice and use it to line the pudding basin, saving one slice for the lid.

3. Bring the cream to a simmer, then pour it over the chocolate. Stir gently to emulsify. Fold the cherries into the chocolate ganache and spoon it into the pudding basin. Top with the last slice of soaked bread then cover the basin with cling film.

4. Put a small board on top of the pudding basin and weigh it down with a can, then leave it to chill in the fridge for at least 4 hours.

5. When you're ready to serve, invert the pudding onto a plate and peel away the cling film.

TOP TIP

Serve the pudding with clotted cream for an extra touch of luxury.

Apple Cake

SERVES 6

PREPARATION TIME 15 MINUTES

COOKING TIME 2–3 HOURS

INGREDIENTS

200 g / 7 oz / ¾ cup caster (superfine) sugar
1 large egg
3 tbsp sunflower oil
1 tsp vanilla extract
150 g / 5 ½ oz / 1 cup plain (all-purpose) flour
½ tsp bicarbonate of (baking) soda
½ tsp baking powder
½ tsp ground cinnamon
3 apples, peeled, cored and sliced

METHOD

1. Whisk the sugar, egg, oil and vanilla extract together with an electric whisk for 4 minutes or until thick. Stir in the flour, raising agents and cinnamon together, then fold in the egg mixture and apples.

2. Butter the inside of a small slow cooker and scrape in the cake mixture. Put the lid on and bake on medium for 2 hours.

3. Test the cake by inserting a skewer into the centre; if it comes out clean, the cake is done. Otherwise, continue to cook and check again every 30 minutes until it is ready.

4. Leave to cool completely before cutting and serving.

TOP TIP

Try using pears instead of apples and add a handful of sultanas.

Individual Bread and Butter Puddings

MAKES 4

PREPARATION TIME 20 MINUTES

COOKING TIME 1 HOUR

INGREDIENTS

- thick slices white bread
- 3 tbsp butter, softened
- tbsp sultanas
- 250 ml / 9 fl. oz / 1 cup milk
- 200 ml / 7 fl. oz / ¾ cup double (heavy) cream
- large egg yolks
- 75 g / 2 ½ oz / ⅓ cup caster (superfine) sugar
- lemon, zest finely grated
- nutmeg to grate

METHOD

1. Spread the bread with butter and cut each piece into four triangles. Butter four small baking dishes and layer up the bread inside with the sultanas.

2. Whisk the milk, cream, eggs, sugar and lemon zest together and divide it between the dishes. Leave to soak for 10 minutes.

3. Preheat the oven to 150°C (130°C fan) / 300F / gas 2. Bake the puddings for 1 hour or until the custard is just set with a slight wobble. Grate over a little nutmeg and serve hot or cold.

TOP TIP

Spread the bread with marmalade and replace the raisins with chocolate chips.

Fig and Apple Crumble

SERVES 4

PREPARATION TIME 15 MINUTES

COOKING TIME 1 HOUR 30 MINUTES

INGREDIENTS

4 eating apples, peeled, cored and diced
4 figs, cut into quarters
2 tbsp caster (superfine) sugar
75 g / 2 ½ oz / ⅓ cup butter
50 g / 1 ¾ oz / ⅓ cup plain (all-purpose) flour
25 g / 1 oz / ¼ cup ground almonds
40 g / 1 ½ oz / ¼ cup light brown sugar
50 g / 1 ¾ oz / ½ cup porridge oats

METHOD

1. Preheat the oven to 160°C (140°C fan) / 325F / gas 3.

2. Mix the apples with the figs and caster sugar in a baking dish. Cover the dish with foil and bake in the oven for 1 hour.

3. Take the fruit out of the oven and increase the temperature to 180°C (160°C fan) / 350F / gas 4.

4. Rub the butter into the flour and stir in the ground almonds, sugar and oats. Take a handful of the topping and squeeze it into a clump, then crumble it over the fruit.

5. Repeat with the rest of the crumble mixture, then bake for 30 minutes or until the topping is golden brown.

TOP TIP

Try using stoned dates in place of the figs.

Crème Caramel

SERVES 6

PREPARATION TIME **30 MINUTES**

COOKING TIME **3 HOURS**

CHILLING TIME **4 HOURS**

INGREDIENTS

175 g / 6 oz / ¾ cup caster (superfine) sugar

tbsp butter, softened

00 ml / 1 pint / 2 ½ cups whole milk

large eggs

tsp vanilla bean paste

METHOD

1. Preheat the slow cooker to low.

2. Put 150 g / 5 oz / ⅔ cup of the sugar in a heavy-based saucepan and heat gently until it starts to turn liquid at the edges. Continue to heat and swirl the pan until the sugar has melted and turned golden brown. Divide the caramel between six ramekin dishes and leave to set, then butter the sides of the ramekins.

3. Whisk the milk, eggs and vanilla bean paste with the remaining sugar and divide between the ramekins. Cover each ramekin with buttered foil. Sit the ramekins in the slow cooker and pour enough boiling water around them to come halfway up the sides.

4. Cook on low for 3 hours or until the crème caramels are just set with a slight wobble in the centre. Remove the ramekins from the slow cooker and chill for 4 hours or overnight.

5. Give the ramekins a vigorous shake to loosen the crème caramels, then turn each one out onto a plate.

TOP TIP

Try flavouring the custard with lemon zest instead of vanilla.

189

Sweet Apricot Tagine

SERVES 2

PREPARATION TIME 10 MINUTES

COOKING TIME 1 HOUR

INGREDIENTS

10 apricots
4 tbsp honey
½ tsp almond extract
½ tsp orange flower water
100 ml / 3 ½ fl. oz / ½ cup apple juice
2 tbsp flaked (slivered) almonds

METHOD

1. Preheat the oven to 150°C (130°C fan) / 300F / gas 2.

2. Arrange the apricots in two individual tagines. Stir the honey, almond extract and orange flower water into the apple juice, then spoon it over the apricots.

3. Put the lids on the tagines and transfer them to the oven. Bake for 1 hour or until the apricots are tender through to the stones. Sprinkle with almonds and serve immediately.

TOP TIP

This recipe is also delicious made with peaches.

Pecan and Maple Syrup Cheesecake

SERVES 8

PREPARATION TIME 30 MINUTES

COOKING TIME 3 HOURS

CHILLING TIME 2 HOURS

INGREDIENTS

200 g / 7 oz / ¾ cups digestive biscuits, crushed
50 g / 1 ¾ oz / ¼ cup butter, melted
600 g / 1 lb 5 oz / 2 ¾ cups cream cheese
150 ml / 5 fl. oz / ⅔ cup soured cream
2 large eggs, plus 1 egg yolk
2 tbsp plain (all-purpose) flour
100 ml / 3 ½ fl. oz / ⅓ cup maple syrup
75 g / 2 ½ oz / ⅓ cup caster (superfine) sugar

For the pecan topping

3 tbsp maple syrup
75 g / 2 ½ oz / ⅔ cup pecan nuts, roughly chopped

METHOD

1. Mix the biscuit crumbs with the butter and press into an even layer in the bottom of a spring-form cake tin that will fit inside your slow cooker.

2. Whisk together the cream cheese, soured cream, eggs, egg yolk and flour until smooth. Divide the mixture between two bowls, then beat the maple syrup into one half. Pour it into the tin and level the surface. Beat the caster sugar into the second bowl, then spoon it into the tin and level the surface.

3. Put a rack into the bottom of your slow cooker and add 2.5 cm (1 in) of boiling water, then position the cake tin on top. Cover the top of the slow cooker with three layers of kitchen paper before putting on the lid. The paper will collect the condensed steam and stop it from dripping onto the cheesecake.

4. Cook on high for 2 hours, then turn off the slow cooker and leave to cook in the residual heat without lifting the lid for 1 hour.

5. Take the cheesecake out of the slow cooker and leave to cool to room temperature before chilling for at least 2 hours.

6. Stir the maple syrup and pecans together and drizzle over the cheesecake before serving.

TOP TIP
If you can't find pecan nuts, use walnuts instead.

DESSERTS

Orange Crème Caramel

SERVES 6

PREPARATION TIME 20 MINUTES

COOKING TIME 3 HOURS

CHILLING TIME 4 HOURS

INGREDIENTS

175 g / 6 oz / ¾ cup caster (superfine) sugar
1 tbsp butter, softened
500 ml / 17 ½ fl. oz / 2 cups whole milk
100 ml / 3 ½ fl. oz / ½ cup orange juice, sieved
4 large eggs
1 tsp orange zest, finely grated
1 tbsp Cointreau

METHOD

1. Preheat the slow cooker to low.

2. Put 150 g / 5 oz / ⅔ cup of the sugar in a heavy-based saucepan and heat gently until it starts to turn liquid at the edges. Continue to heat and swirl the pan until the sugar has all melted and turned golden brown.

3. Divide the caramel between six ramekin dishes and leave to set, then butter the sides of the ramekins.

4. Whisk the rest of the ingredients with the remaining of sugar and divide between the ramekins. Cover each ramekin with buttered foil. Sit the ramekins in the slow cooker and pour enough boiling water around them to come halfway up the sides.

5. Cook on low for 3 hours or until the crème caramels are just set with a slight wobble in the centre. Remove the ramekins from the slow cooker and chill for 4 hours or overnight.

6. Give the ramekins a vigorous shake to loosen the crème caramels, then turn each one out onto a plate.

TOP TIP
Try adding a pinch of Cayenne pepper to the custard for a spicy kick.

Stewed Cherries with Fromage Frais

SERVES 4

PREPARATION TIME **10 MINUTES**

COOKING TIME **1 HOUR 30 MINUTES**

INGREDIENTS

450 g / 1 lb / 2 ½ cups cherries, stoned

100 g / 3 ½ oz / ½ cup caster (superfine) sugar

100 ml / 3 ½ fl. oz / ½ cup rosé wine

3 tbsp kirsch

½ tsp almond essence

450 g / 1 lb / 2 cups natural fromage frais

75 g / 2 ½ oz / ¾ cup icing (confectioners') sugar

METHOD

1. Stir the cherries and caster sugar into the wine in a small slow cooker. Cover and cook on medium for 1 hour 30 minutes or until the cherries are starting to collapse. Stir in the kirsch and almond essence and leave to cool.

2. Beat the fromage frais with the icing sugar until smooth then divide between four serving bowls or glasses.

3. Spoon the stewed cherries over the top and serve immediately.

TOP TIP

Spice up the cherries with a whole star anise while they're poaching.

Peach and Pomegranate Tagine

SERVES 2

PREPARATION TIME 10 MINUTES

COOKING TIME 45 MINUTES

INGREDIENTS

3 peaches, quartered and stoned
2 tbsp honey
1 tsp rose water
100 ml / 3 ½ fl. oz / ½ cup pomegranate juice
½ pomegranate

METHOD

1. Preheat the oven to 150°C (130°C fan) / 300F / gas 2.

2. Arrange the peach quarters in two individual tagines. Stir the honey and rose water into the pomegranate juice, then spoon it over the peaches.

3. Put the lids on the tagines and transfer them to the oven. Bake for 45 minutes or until the peaches are tender.

4. Hold the pomegranate over a bowl and hit the rounded side with a wooden spoon to release the seeds. Sprinkle the seeds over the peaches and serve immediately.

TOP TIP
Try adding a few chopped stoned dates to the tagine.

Peach Compote with Poached Meringue

SERVES 6

PREPARATION TIME 20 MINUTES

COOKING TIME 1 HOUR 30 MINUTES

INGREDIENTS

12 ripe peaches, peeled, stoned and chopped
1 lemon, juiced
4 tbsp caster (superfine) sugar
2 tbsp brandy

For the poached meringue
500 ml / 1 pint / 2 ½ cups milk
4 large egg whites
110 g / 4 oz / ½ cup caster (superfine) sugar
2 tbsp toasted flaked (slivered) almonds

METHOD

1. Toss the peaches with the lemon juice, sugar and brandy in a slow cooker. Put on the lid and cook on low for 1 hour 30 minutes or until the fruit has started to break down. Leave the compote chunky or use a stick blender to purée the fruit.

2. Put the milk in a saucepan with 500 ml / 17 fl. oz / 2 cups of boiling water and bring to a gentle simmer.

3. Whisk the egg whites until stiff, then gradually add the sugar, whisking until the mixture is thick and shiny.

4. Transfer 6 tbsp of the mixture to the simmering milk and poach the meringues for 10 minutes, turning halfway through. Transfer the meringues to a wire rack and leave to steam dry for a few minutes.

5. Serve the compote hot or chilled and top with the meringues and a sprinkle of almonds.

TOP TIP

This compote is also delicious made with apricots.

Poached Fruit with Raclette Crumble Topping

SERVES 4–6

PREPARATION TIME 30 MINUTES

COOKING TIME 1 HOUR 30 MINUTES

INGREDIENTS

2 eating apples, cored and cut into wedges
2 pears, peeled, cored and cut into wedges
1 peach, peeled, stoned and cut into wedges
500 ml / 17 ½ fl. oz / 2 cups apple juice
75 g / 2 ½ oz / ⅓ cup butter
50 g / 1 ¾ oz / ⅓ cup plain (all-purpose) flour
25 g / 1 oz / ½ cup ground almonds
40 g / 1 ½ oz / ¼ cup light brown sugar

METHOD

1. Put the fruit in a slow cooker and pour over the juice. Cook on medium for 1 hour 30 minutes or until the fruit is tender, but still holding its shape.

2. Rub the butter into the flour and stir in the ground almonds and sugar, then transfer the mixture to a serving bowl.

3. Set a raclette grill in the middle of the table and put it on to heat. Each diner can then put a few pieces of fruit in a raclette tray and sprinkle with the crumble topping before cooking it under the raclette grill.

TOP TIP

If you don't have a raclette, toast the crumble under a hot grill.

Pear, Orange and Cinnamon Tagine

SERVES **4**

PREPARATION TIME **10 MINUTES**

COOKING TIME **2 HOURS**

INGREDIENTS

5 pears, peeled, cored and quartered
2 oranges
4 tbsp honey
1 cinnamon stick

METHOD

1. Preheat the oven to 150°C (130°C fan) / 300F / gas 2.

2. Arrange the pear quarters in four individual tagines. Cut four slices from one of the oranges and tuck a slice into each tagine, then squeeze over the juice from the remaining oranges and drizzle with honey. Break the cinnamon stick into shards and sprinkle a little into each tagine.

3. Put the lids on the tagines and transfer them to the oven. Bake for 2 hour or until the pears are really tender.

TOP TIP
Try adding a few slices of fresh root ginger for a spicy kick.

Poached Apples with Sesame Caramel

SERVES 4

PREPARATION TIME 30 MINUTES

COOKING TIME 1 HOUR 30 MINUTES

INGREDIENTS

4 apples, peeled, cored and halved
500 ml / 17 ½ fl. oz / 2 cups apple juice
1 tbsp butter
1 tsp sesame oil
½ tbsp sesame seeds

METHOD

1. Arrange the apples cut side down in a single layer in a slow cooker. Pour over the apple juice then cook on medium for 1 hour 30 minutes or until the apples are tender to the point of a knife.

2. Drain the apples through a colander and collect the juice in a saucepan. Boil the juice over a high heat until it has reduced to a syrupy consistency, then whisk in the butter and sesame oil to make a shiny caramel sauce.

3. Divide the apples between four bowls, then drizzle over the sauce and sprinkle with sesame seeds.

TOP TIP
Serve the apples warm with cold vanilla ice cream.

Strawberry and Almond Cheesecake

SERVES 8

PREPARATION TIME 30 MINUTES

COOKING TIME 3 HOURS

CHILLING TIME 2 HOURS

INGREDIENTS

200 g / 7 oz / ¾ cup sweet oat biscuits, crushed

50 g / 1 ¾ oz / ¼ cup butter, melted

600 g / 1 lb 5 oz / 2 ¾ cups cream cheese

150 ml / 5 fl. oz / ⅔ cup soured cream

2 large eggs, plus 1 egg yolk

½ tsp almond essence

2 tbsp plain (all-purpose) flour

150 g / 5 ½ oz / ⅔ cup caster (superfine) sugar

75 g / 2 ½ oz / 1 cup flaked (slivered) almonds

200 g / 7 oz / 1 ⅓ cups strawberries, quartered

METHOD

1. Mix the biscuit crumbs with the butter and press into an even layer in the bottom of a spring-form cake tin that will fit inside your slow cooker.

2. Whisk together the cream cheese, soured cream, eggs, egg yolk, almond essence, flour, sugar and flaked almonds until smoothly combined.

3. Put a rack into the bottom of your slow cooker and add 2.5 cm (1 in) of boiling water, then position the cake tin on top. Cover the top of the slow cooker with three layers of kitchen paper before putting on the lid. The paper will collect the condensed steam and stop it from dripping onto the cheesecake.

4. Cook on high for 2 hours, then turn off the slow cooker and leave to cook in the residual heat without lifting the lid for 1 hour.

5. Take the cheesecake out of the slow cooker and leave to cool to room temperature before chilling for at least 2 hours.

6. Pile the strawberries on top before serving.

TOP TIP

Try using stoned poached cherries in place of the strawberries.

DESSERTS

Lavender and Honey Rice Pudding

METHOD

1. Butter the inside of a slow cooker. Stir all of the ingredients together, then tip the mixture into the slow cooker.

2. Cook on high for 3 hours, stirring once every hour.

3. Spoon into warm bowls and serve with extra honey for drizzling over.

SERVES **4**

PREPARATION TIME **5 MINUTES**

COOKING TIME **3 HOURS**

INGREDIENTS

50 g / 1 ¾ oz / ¼ cup butter, plus extra
    for greasing
1.2 litres / 2 pints / 4 ½ cups whole milk
3 sprigs of lavender, stems removed
110 g / 4 oz / ½ cup short-grain rice
75 g / 2 ½ oz / ¼ cup runny honey, plus extra
    to serve

TOP TIP
Try adding the finely grated zest of an orange for added zing.

Lemon Soufflés

SERVES 4

PREPARATION TIME **20 MINUTES**

COOKING TIME **1 HOUR**

INGREDIENTS

1 tbsp butter
3 tbsp caster (superfine) sugar
2 large egg whites
1 tbsp cornflour (cornstarch)
100 g / 3 ½ oz / ½ cup lemon curd

METHOD

1. Put a rack inside a slow cooker and add 2.5 cm (1 in) of boiling water, then set it to high.

2. Butter four mini pudding basins and use 1 tbsp of the sugar to coat the insides.

3. Whisk the egg whites with an electric whisk until stiff, then whisk in the rest of the sugar. Stir the cornflour into the lemon curd, then fold in the egg whites.

4. Spoon the mixture into the prepared pudding basins, then transfer them to the slow cooker. Lay three layers of kitchen paper over the top of the slow cooker, then cover with a lid to absorb the steam.

5. Cook for 1 hour or until the soufflés are only just set in the centres. Serve immediately.

TOP TIP

Top with a scoop of vanilla ice cream and a drizzle of lemon curd before serving.

Slow-cooked knickerbocker glory

METHOD

1. Mix the fruit with the sugar and wine in a slow cooker. Cover and cook on medium for 1 hour 30 minutes then leave to cool completely.

2. Spoon the fruit and cooking liquor into six tall sundae glasses and top with the ice cream and pistachio nuts.

SERVES 6

PREPARATION TIME 10 MINUTES

COOKING TIME 1 HOUR 30 MINUTES

INGREDIENTS

1 pineapple, peeled and cut into chunks
300 g / 10 ½ oz / 1 ⅔ cups black cherries, stoned
3 pears, peeled, cored and cut into chunks
100 g / 3 ½ oz / ½ cup caster (superfine) sugar
100 ml / 3 ½ fl. oz / ½ cup rosé wine
6 scoops vanilla ice cream
50 g / 1 ¾ oz / ½ cup pistachio nuts, chopped

TOP TIP
Try serving with different ice creams for a change.

Carrot Cake

SERVES 10

PREPARATION TIME 25 MINUTES

COOKING TIME 3 HOURS

INGREDIENTS

175 g / 6 oz / 1 cup soft light brown sugar
2 large eggs
150 ml / 5 fl. oz / ⅔ cup sunflower oil
175 g / 6 oz / 1 ¼ cups plain (all-purpose) flour
3 tsp baking powder
2 tsp ground cinnamon
1 orange, zest finely grated
200 g / 7 oz / 1 ⅔ cups carrots, washed and
    coarsely grated
100 g / 3 ½ oz / ¾ cup walnuts, chopped

For the icing

110 g / 4 oz / ½ cup cream cheese
55 g / 2 oz / ¼ cup butter, softened
110 g / 4 oz / 1 cup icing (confectioners') sugar
1 tsp vanilla extract
2 tbsp walnuts, finely chopped

METHOD

1. Put a rack in the bottom of a slow cooker and add 2.5 cm (1 in) of boiling water.

2. Grease and line a cake tin that will fit inside your slow cooker.

3. Whisk the sugar, eggs and oil together for 3 minutes until thick. Fold in the flour, baking powder and cinnamon, followed by the orange zest, carrots and walnuts.

4. Scrape the mixture into the tin and lower it into the slow cooker. Cook on high for 3 hours or until a skewer inserted in the centre comes out clean. Transfer the cake to a wire rack and leave to cool completely.

5. To make the icing, beat the cream cheese and butter together with a wooden spoon until light and fluffy, then beat in the icing sugar a quarter at a time. Add the vanilla extract then use a whisk the mixture for 2 minutes or until smooth and light.

6. Spread the icing over the cake and sprinkle with walnuts.

TOP TIP
Try using beetroot in place of the carrot.

Poached Pears and Cherries with Herbs

METHOD

1. Put everything in a slow cooker, then cover and cook on medium for 2 hours.

2. Serve warm or chilled.

SERVES 6

PREPARATION TIME 5 MINUTES

COOKING TIME 2 HOURS

INGREDIENTS

4 pears, quartered
200 g / 7 oz / 1 ⅓ cups cherries, stoned and halved
2 tbsp caster (superfine) sugar
1 lemon, juiced
2 sprigs rosemary
2 sprigs thyme

TOP TIP
Use the fruit as a base for a crumble or pie.

Index